THE STAINED GLASS MUSEUM

HIGHLIGHTS FROM THE COLLECTION

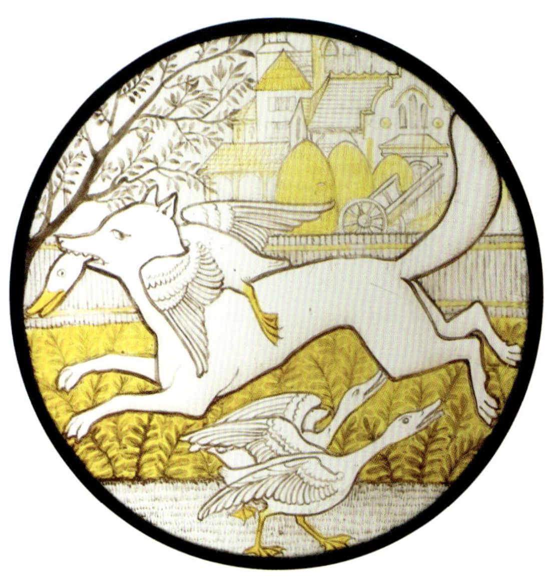

SCALA

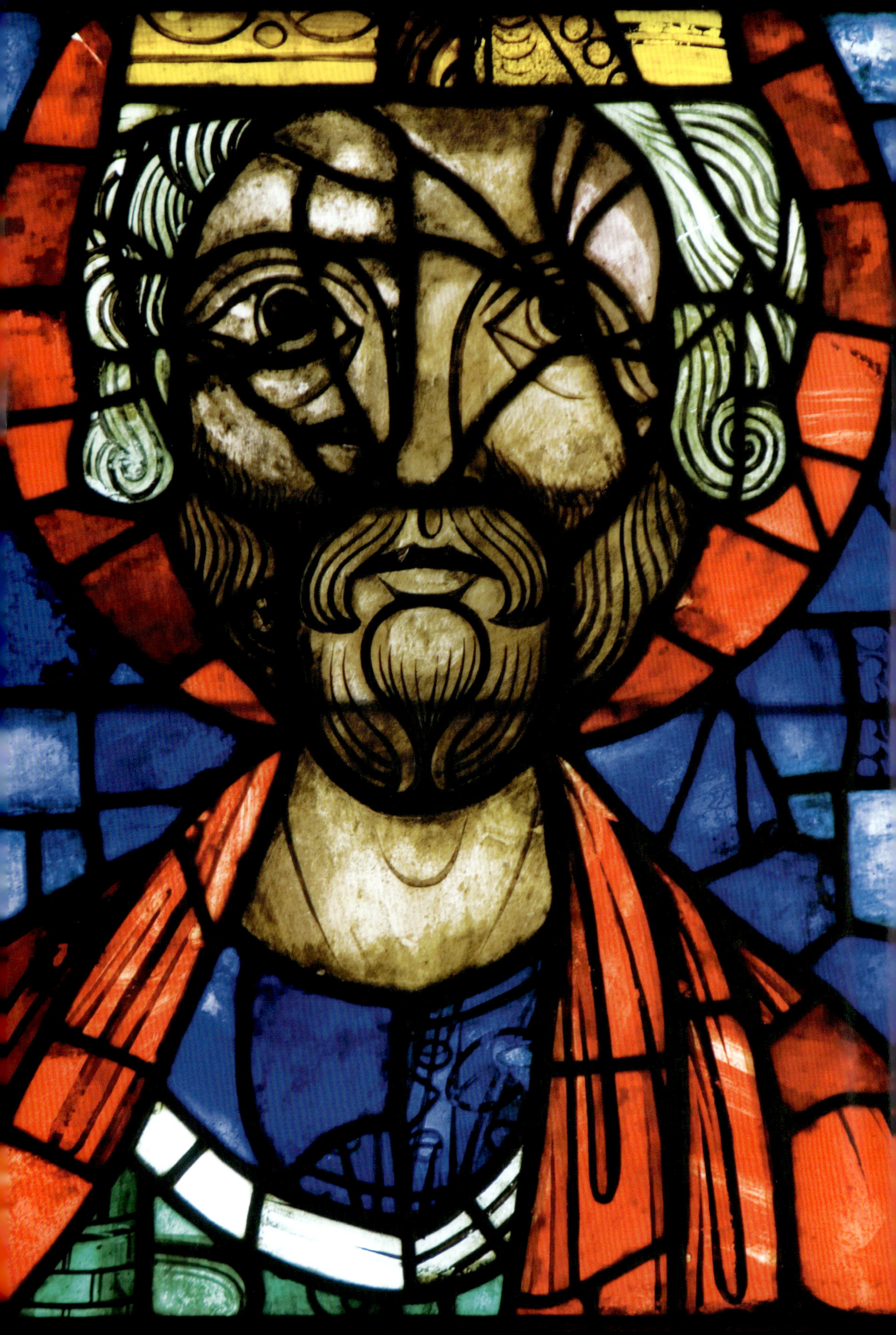

CONTENTS

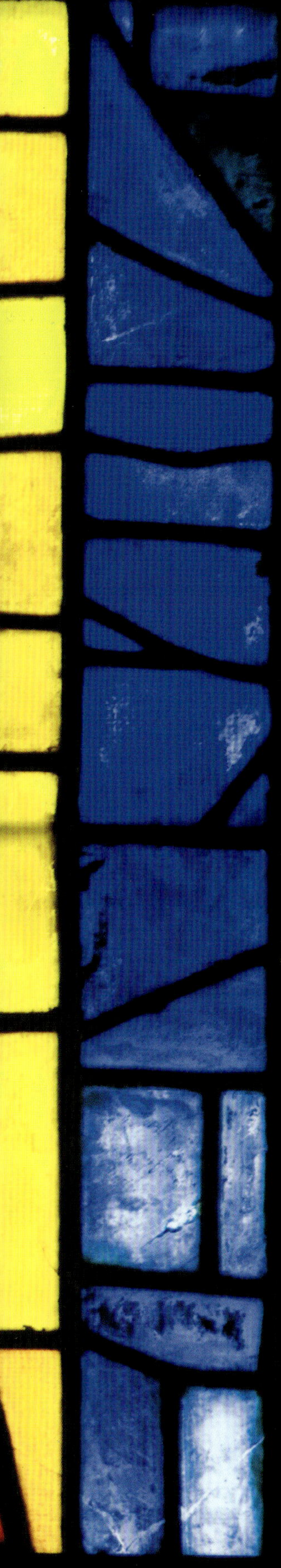
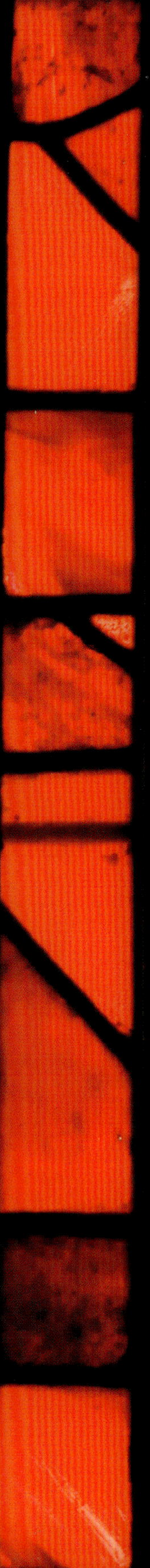

AN ILLUMINATING ART

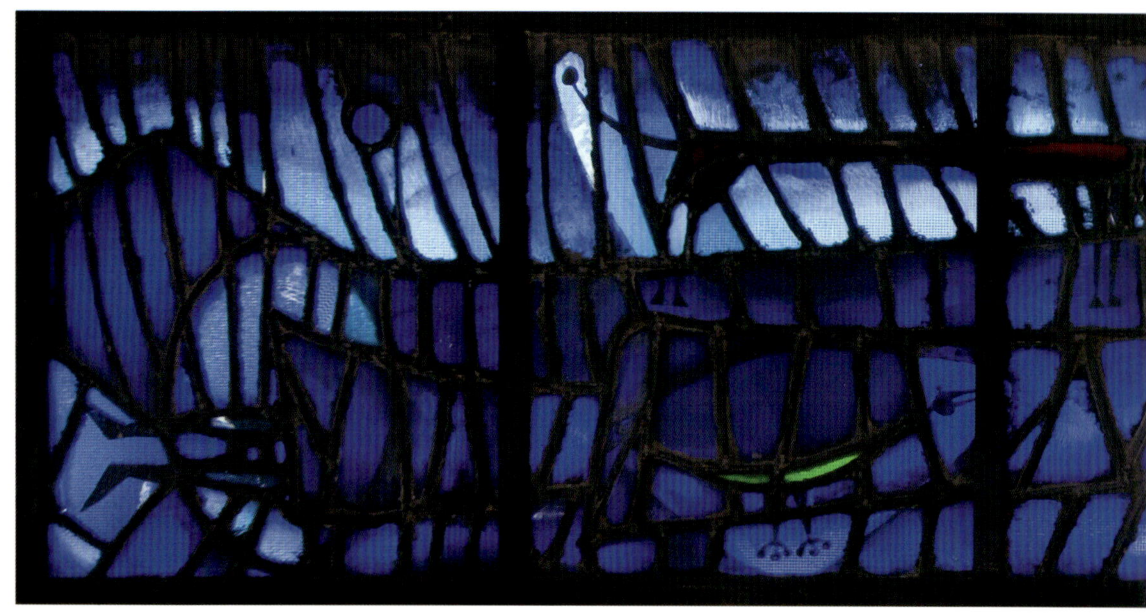

Stained glass is a unique art form that is illuminated by transmitted light, either from the sun or an artificial light source. For several centuries it has been used to glaze windows in a variety of religious and secular buildings. Once almost solely confined to medieval churches and chapels, guildhalls, hospitals and manor houses whose patrons could afford luxurious coloured glass windows, during the 19th and 20th centuries stained glass windows became popular in other places of worship, including synagogues and Nonconformist chapels, as well as civic and domestic buildings. In recent times it has been used to enliven and form part of the main structure of corporate buildings, hotels, community and shopping centres.

The Stained Glass Museum has a nationally significant collection of stained glass panels and windows from the 13th century through to the present day, as well as a number of designs, sketches, cartoons and tools associated with the art and craft, which has been practised in Britain for almost 1,500 years. This guide describes and illustrates some of the highlights from the Museum's growing collection, and provides a visual guide to the stylistic and technical development of stained glass from its ancient origins to the 21st century.

THE ORIGIN AND MAKING OF STAINED GLASS

It is difficult to date precisely when stained glass windows were first made in Britain. However, there is evidence to suggest that some Anglo-Saxon churches were decorated with stained glass. Hundreds of pieces of coloured glass and lead dating to the late 7th century were excavated at Monkwearmouth and Jarrow in Northumbria in the 1970s. Some of the best-preserved pieces were collected together and placed

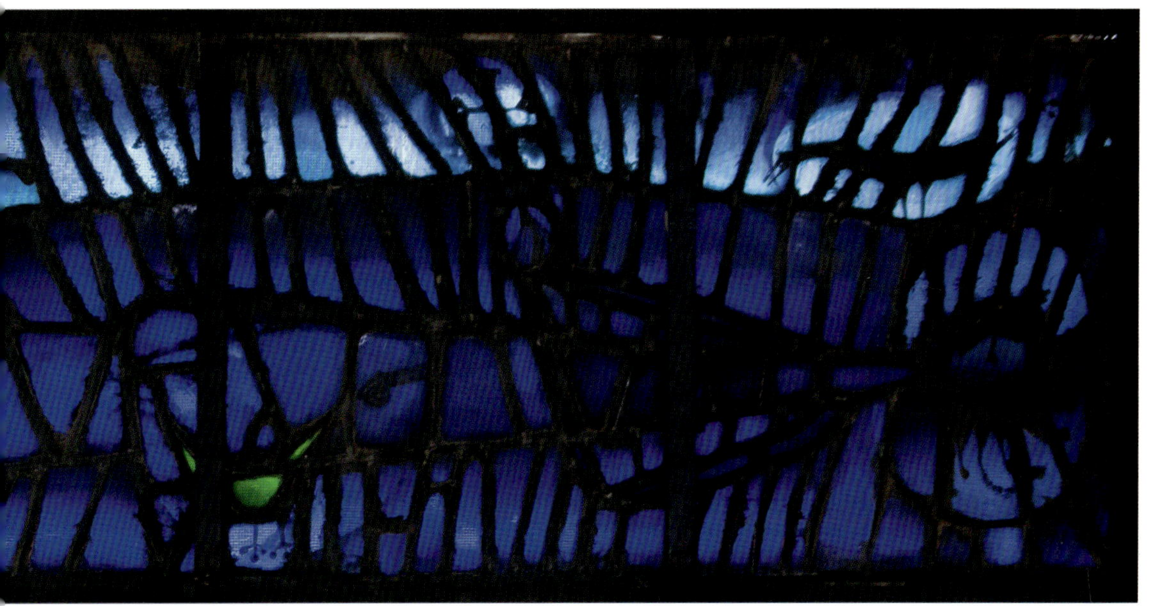

in a window in St Paul's Church, Jarrow. The earliest example of stained glass in situ in the British Isles dates from the 11th century. A window depicting Archangel Michael in All Saints Church, Dalbury, Derbyshire, is thought to date from this period, although such examples are rare. Stained glass windows dating from the 12th century can be seen in both Canterbury Cathedral and York Minster, but the majority of surviving medieval glass in both parish churches and cathedrals dates from the 14th and 15th centuries.

The raw material of glass is formed when sand (silica) is heated at a high temperature. Glass is coloured by the addition of metallic oxides or salts. Whilst hot, molten glass can be manipulated and shaped by tools and a glass blowing iron. There are two main methods of blowing glass into a sheet by *gathering* molten glass on the end of a blowing iron. The 'crown' method involves turning the blowing iron while blowing. The centrifugal force produces a spun disc, thickest in the centre where the blowing iron is joined. Whilst still hot the *crown* is cut away from the blowing iron and left to cool. Using the 'cylinder' technique the molten glass is blown into a balloon-like shape. During the annealing process the ends are cut off and the *muff*, as it is known, is scored down the middle and then re-heated to form a large flattened sheet.

Traditionally, a stained glass window is made of small pieces of coloured sheet glass held together in a lead

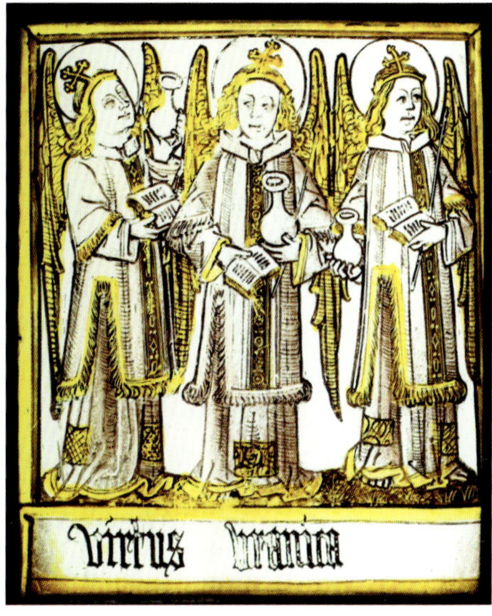

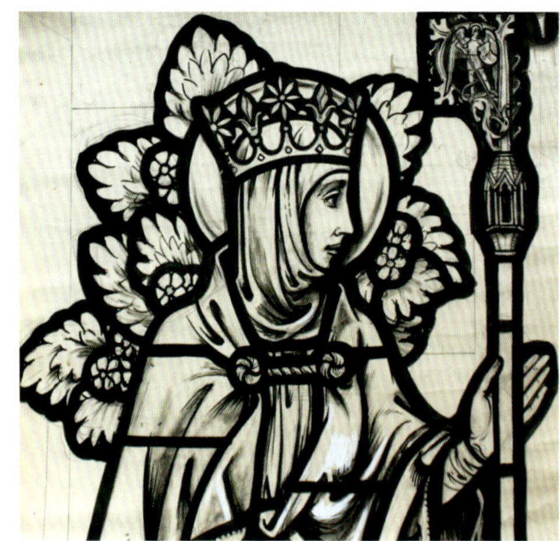

matrix to form a pattern or image in a manner similar to mosaic. Pieces of sheet glass are cut to size with a glass-cutter (in the Middle Ages a hot iron was used) following a full-scale drawing of the design known as a *cartoon*. Details, such as facial features or decorative patterns, can be painted onto the glass using a *glass paint* containing finely ground glass. The paint is 'fixed' to the glass surface by being fired in a kiln up to a temperature of around 650°C. Once cool, the pieces of glass are then reassembled on the workbench for glazing. This process involves fitting moulded lengths of lead, known as *calmes*, around the edges of each piece of glass to hold them in position and then soldering the joints. Finally, the panel is cemented to make it watertight and then it is installed into a framework usually made of iron, called *ferramenta*, which is set within the wall. Stained glass is still made using these traditional methods today, although new techniques have also developed over the centuries.

HISTORY OF THE STAINED GLASS MUSEUM

The Stained Glass Museum was founded in 1972, with the aim of rescuing stained glass windows under threat from destruction and putting them on public display to raise awareness of this unique art and craft. The Stained Glass Museum first opened to the public in 1979 in the north triforium of Ely Cathedral. After a successful 25th Anniversary Appeal, funds were raised to refit the Museum in the south triforium of Ely Cathedral, where it re-opened in 2000.

Since its foundation the Museum has given new life to hundreds of stained glass windows removed from redundant buildings, predominantly churches across the British Isles. Other windows in the Museum's collection, including examples from Europe and North America, have been generously loaned, donated, or purchased with help from funding bodies. Today it is the only museum in the United Kingdom dedicated to the art of stained glass, and has a growing collection. Sadly stained glass remains a threatened part of our cultural and artistic heritage, which, more than ever, requires our care and attention to help preserve it for future generations.

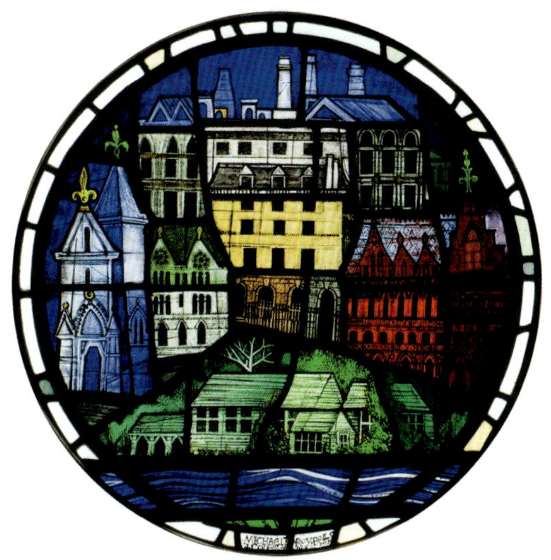

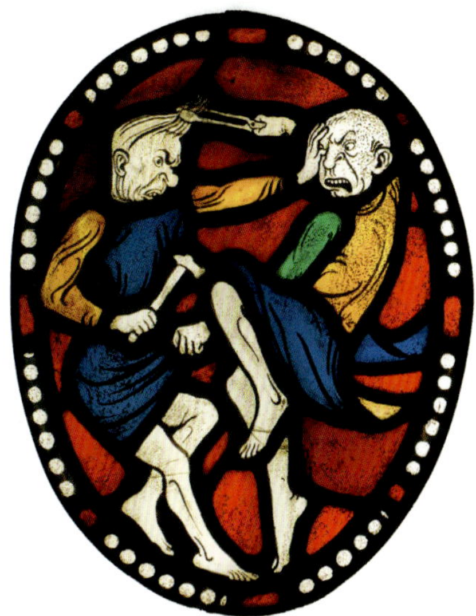

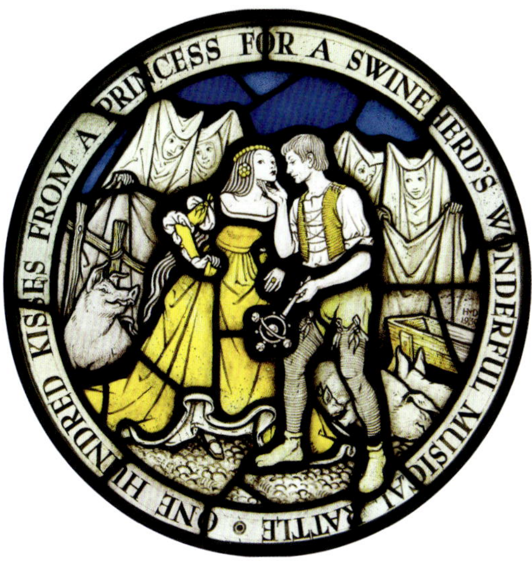
ONE HUNDRED KISSES FROM A PRINCESS FOR A SWINE HERD'S WONDERFUL MUSICAL RATTLE

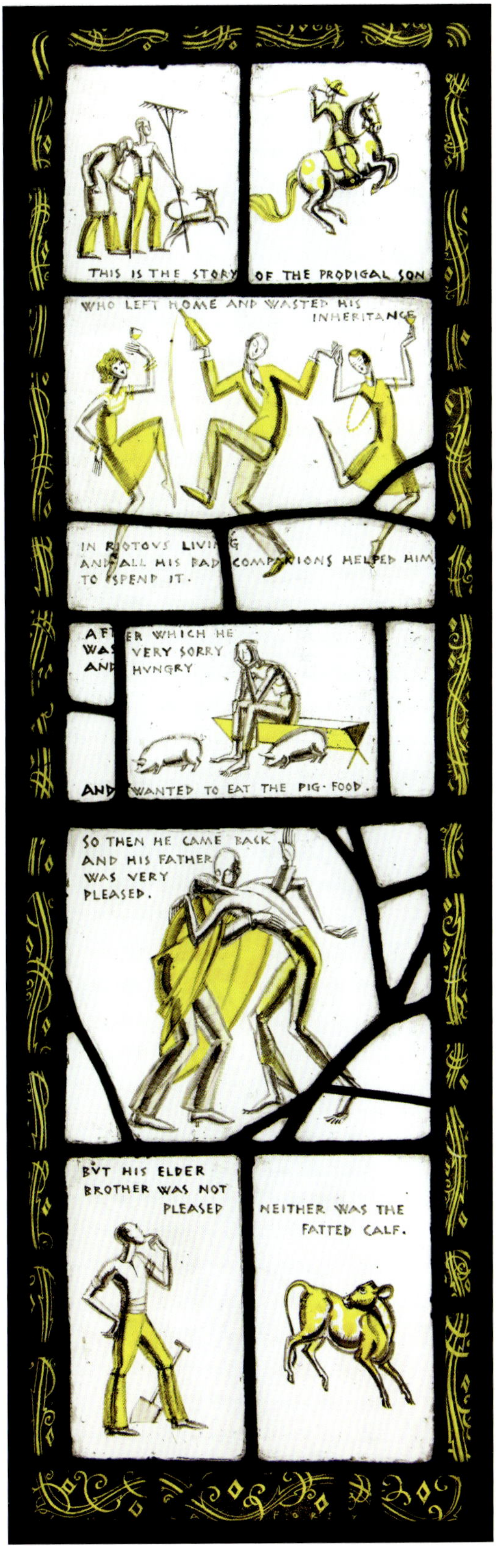

THIS IS THE STORY OF THE PRODIGAL SON
WHO LEFT HOME AND WASTED HIS INHERITANCE
IN RIOTOVS LIVING AND ALL HIS BAD COMPANIONS HELPED HIM TO SPEND IT.
AFTER WHICH HE WAS VERY SORRY AND HVNGRY
AND WANTED TO EAT THE PIG-FOOD.
SO THEN HE CAME BACK AND HIS FATHER WAS VERY PLEASED.
BVT HIS ELDER BROTHER WAS NOT PLEASED
NEITHER WAS THE FATTED CALF.

At a time when few could read, painted windows were used to instruct people in the Christian faith and encourage religious devotion. Many windows illustrated scenes and stories from the Bible and the lives of the saints, who were revered as a source of help in everyday life and as mediators in Heaven. After Christ, the Virgin Mary was the most venerated and thousands of stained glass images were made of her. Unpainted glass with very little colour, arranged in geometric designs, provided cheaper windows for poorer churches and was also favoured in the churches of the austere Cistercian monks. In contrast, rich donors, anxious to be remembered in the prayers of the faithful, paid for expensive windows, which sometimes included their family arms and 'portraits' accompanied by images of their favourite saints.

Medieval stained glass evolved with the Gothic architectural styles of the Middle Ages. From about 1280, figures and scenes were usually arranged under Gothic canopies and within borders, which were filled with foliage, heraldry and fabulous beasts. By the end of the medieval period, a wide range of coloured glass was available to stained glass artists, much of which was imported into Britain from the glass houses of Normandy and the Rhineland. Painting techniques developed rapidly, achieving great realism by the early 1500s. From about 1310, silver stain (or yellow stain), a pigment made from a silver compound, allowed the surface of plain white glass to be richly decorated. This technique was especially important in the making of small roundels and diamond-shaped quarries, and enabled more sophisticated designs. By the early 1500s a reddish enamel colour, called sanguine, also began to be used to colour the surface of glass.

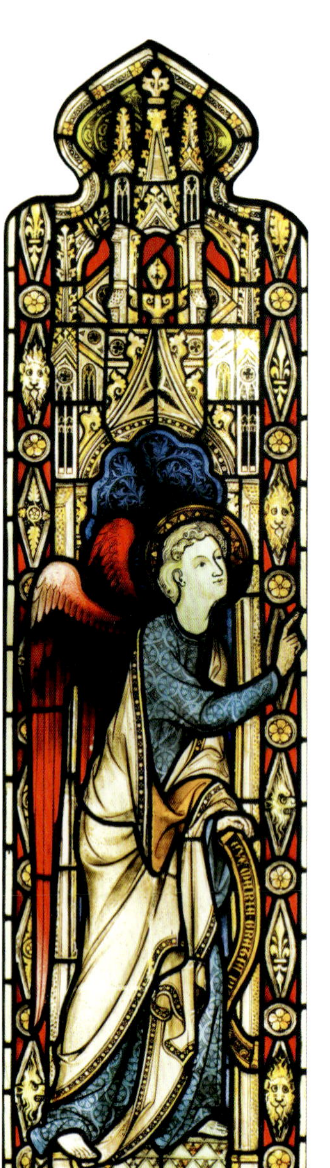

THE ANNUNCIATION TO THE VIRGIN *c.*1340
English artist (West Midlands), restored by Hardman & Co., 1866

Devotion to the Virgin Mary was universal in the Middle Ages and particularly strong in England, believed to be under her special protection. This window is one of the finest examples in English glass painting of the 'Decorated' Gothic style. Silver stain, introduced around the beginning of the 14th century, is used to decorate the Virgin's hair and to pick out many of the canopy details.

Glass by this medieval workshop has been identified in Bristol, Worcester and Oxford cathedrals, as well as many churches in the West Midlands and Severn Valley. In 1866 the windows at Hadzor were sensitively and skilfully restored by the Birmingham firm of John Hardman & Co., which made the figure of Gabriel to match.

From the church of St John the Baptist, Hadzor, Worcestershire. Donated by the Diocese of Worcester, 1976. (1976.4.1,2)

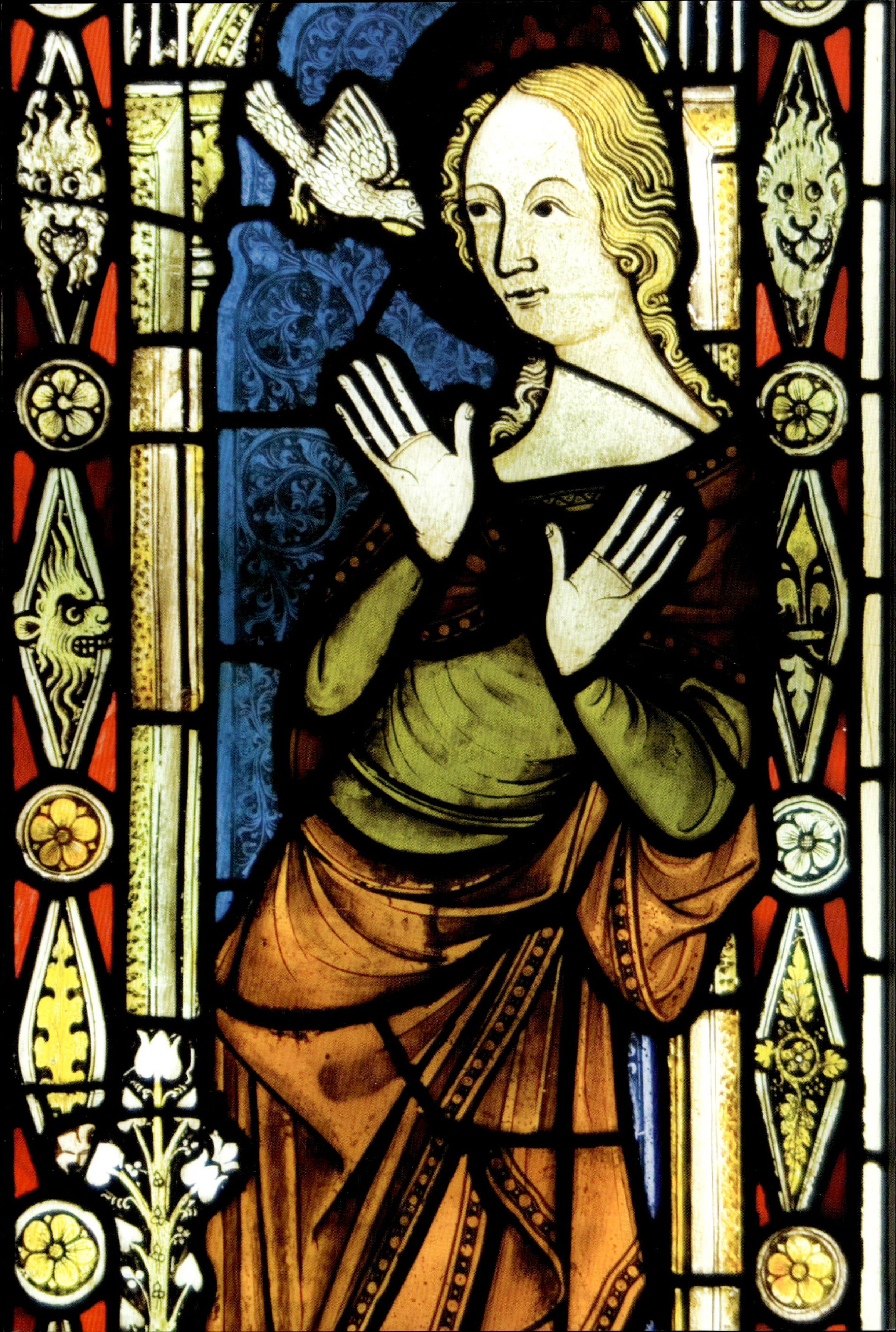

BUST OF A KING *c.*1210
French artist

This bust of a royal saint or Old Testament king, wearing a crown and robe, was once part of a monumental figure. It came from the side windows in the clerestory of the choir of Soissons Cathedral, which contained enthroned figures of prophets and apostles in two tiers. Begun in the late 12th century and brought into use by 1212, the choir at Soissons was a key building in the evolution of the High Gothic architectural style and one of the first cathedrals to include giant figural stained glass windows so characteristic of these great churches. Several windows were removed from the building for restoration in 1882, but ended up being sold and can today be seen in several museum collections across the world.

From Soissons Cathedral, France. Purchased with assistance of the Art Fund, the V&A Purchase Grant Fund, Sam Fogg and the Friends of the Stained Glass Museum, 2003. (2003.3)

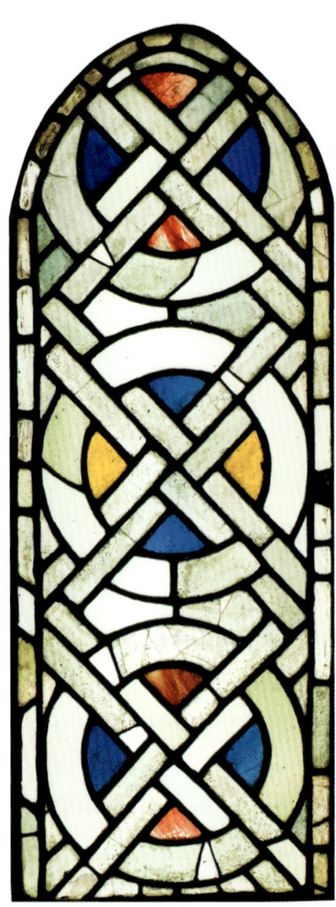

GEOMETRIC GRISAILLE *c.*1200–1250
English artist

Despite its age, this 13th-century panel retains much of its original medieval lead and glass. The rough surface of the lead, cast in moulds, has been planed, giving it a distinctive faceted appearance. The glass is unpainted and therefore relies on the pattern of the leads for its decorative effect. This kind of simple glazing, using predominantly white, or clear, glass is known as grisaille. It is often associated with Cistercian churches, as it expressed the simplicity of the Cistercian monastic ideal. It was also popular wherever more light or a cheaper form of glazing was required.

Original location unknown. Acquired by the studio of James Powell & Sons, probably in the 19th century. Purchased with assistance from The Art Fund, The V&A Purchase Grant Fund and The Sue Pitt Appeal, 2005. (1990.4)

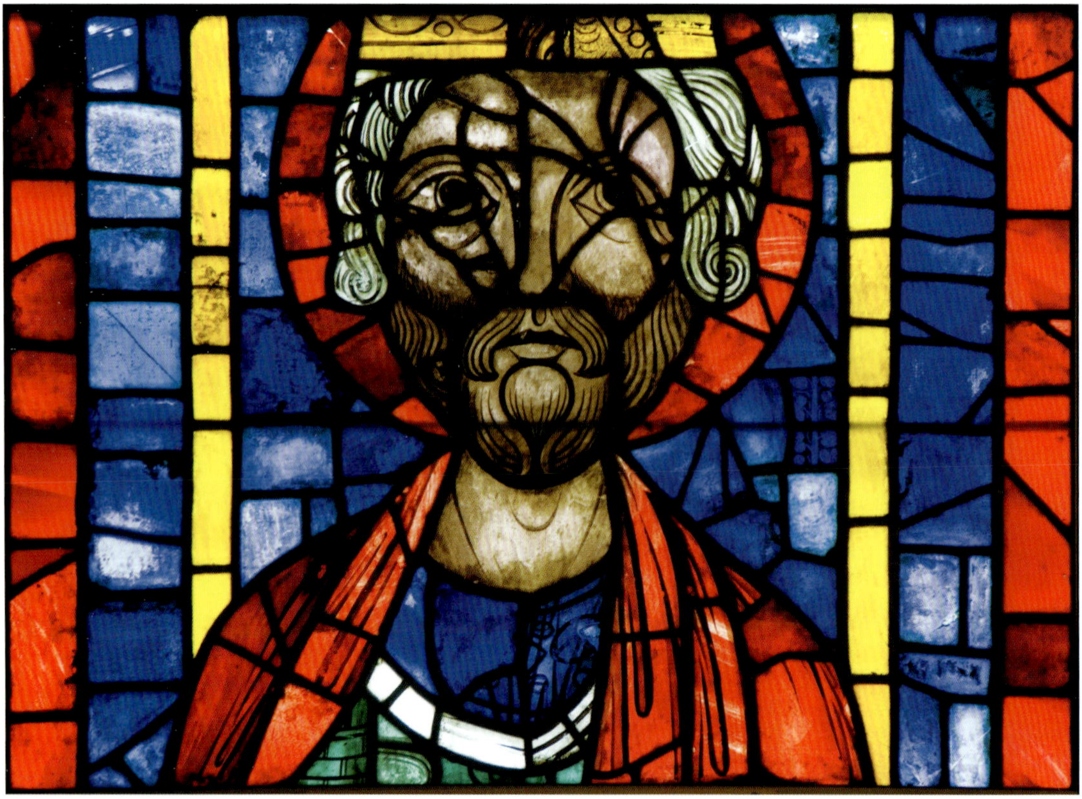

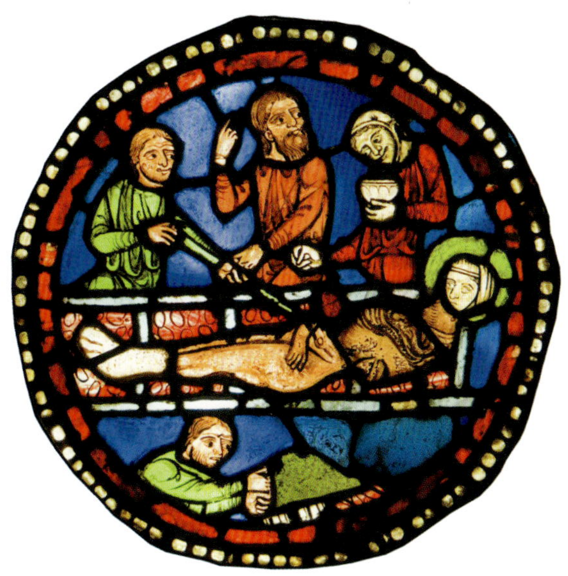

French artist

This roundel comes from a medallion window depicting events in the life of St Vincent; and is thought to have been made for a church in Burgundy, France. Such narrative windows were one of the outstanding achievements of Gothic glass painters. Roundels like this were arranged in complex geometric patterns surrounded by luxuriant foliage decorations. Well-known 12th- and 13th-century examples survive in cathedrals such as Chartres and Canterbury but are rare outside the greater churches.

St Vincent suffered grievously for his Christian beliefs and is shown here being roasted on a gridiron. A figure beneath fans the flames with bellows, while other torturers pierce his body and rub salt into his wounds. In the early 20th century these roundels were displayed in a house in Berkshire. Like much continental glass in Britain, they were probably acquired by a British collector in the late 18th or 19th century.

Original location in France, perhaps Burgundy. On loan from the REME Museum of Technology, 2003. (L2003.7.1)

ST CATHERINE AND ST LAWRENCE *c.*1310–30
English artist (East Anglia)

The patron saint of students, scientists, theologians and wheelwrights, St Catherine of Alexandria was a popular figure throughout medieval Europe. This depiction, with the spiked wheel on which she was tortured, is typical of the many thousands of images in cathedrals and parish churches in medieval Britain.

Lawrence was martyred in AD 258, during the persecutions of the Roman Emperor Valerian. Like St Vincent, he was said to have been roasted on a gridiron, although this grisly detail may not be founded on historical fact.

The style of glass painting shown in these two panels flourished in the period *c.*1280–1350, with figures positioned under decorative canopies in the Gothic style.

From the church of St Andrew, Wood Walton, Cambridgeshire. On loan from the Friends of Friendless Churches, 1980.
(L1980.2.1 and L1980.2.2)

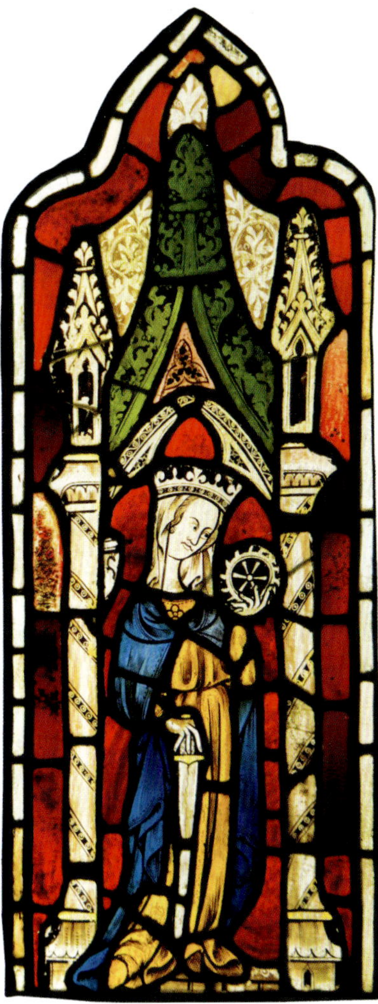
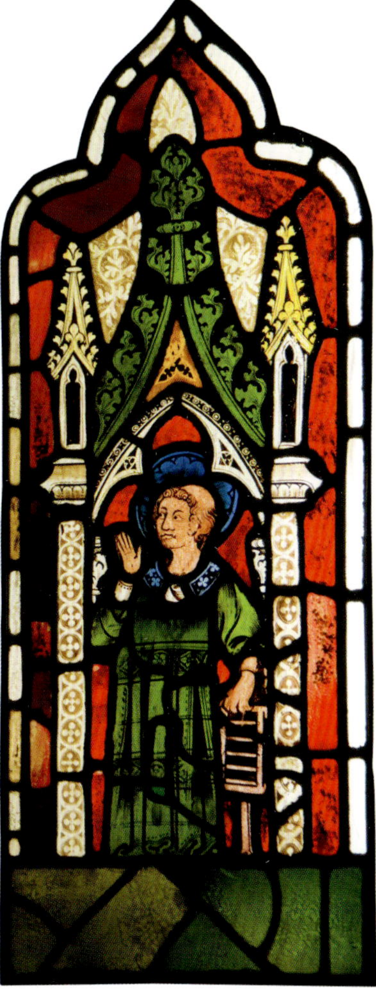

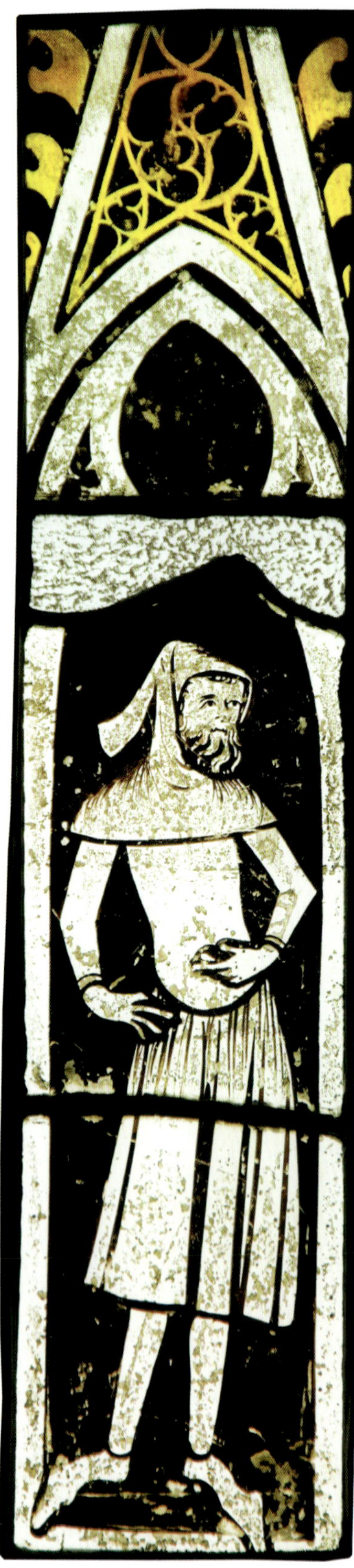

PEASANT FIGURE *c.*1340–49
English artist (East Anglia)

Begun in 1321, the Lady Chapel of Ely Cathedral was once richly coloured, with stained glass and painted and gilded stone sculpture depicting the life and miracles of the Virgin Mary, making it among the most sumptuously decorated interiors in medieval England. Considered superstitious by Protestant reformers, the imagery was badly damaged at the Reformation and only a few pieces of the glazing scheme have survived. This small figure of a peasant, rarely depicted in medieval art, originally occupied a place in a decorated architectural canopy in one of the windows of the Lady Chapel.

From the Lady Chapel, Ely Cathedral. On loan from the Dean and Chapter of Ely Cathedral, 1991. (L1991.4)

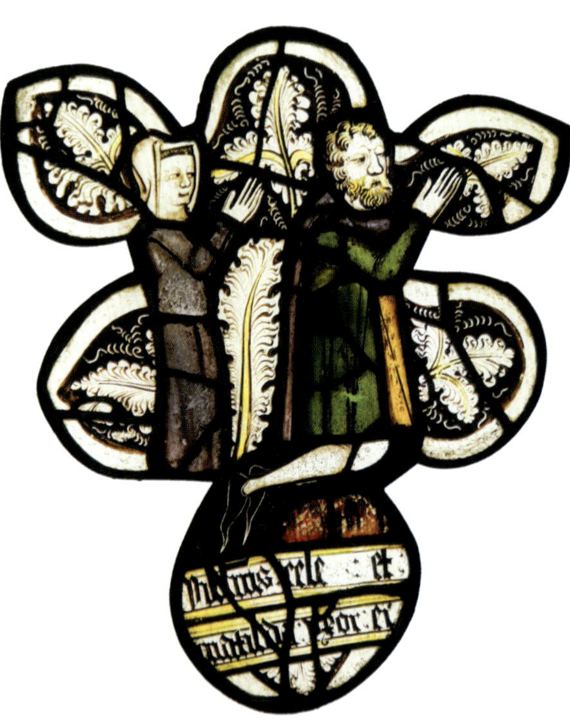

DONORS WILLIAM AND MATILDA CELE *c.*1350–1400
English artist (East Anglia)

From the middle of the 13th century donor figures were often depicted in the stained glass windows they had paid for, sometimes alongside the sacred figures. Nothing is known of the lives of William and Matilda Celes, although their role as patrons has ensured that their names are still remembered centuries after their deaths. This fine example of 14th-century glass painting is believed to have come from a parish church in Suffolk.

Original location in Suffolk. On loan from the Victoria and Albert Museum, 2004. (L2004.2)

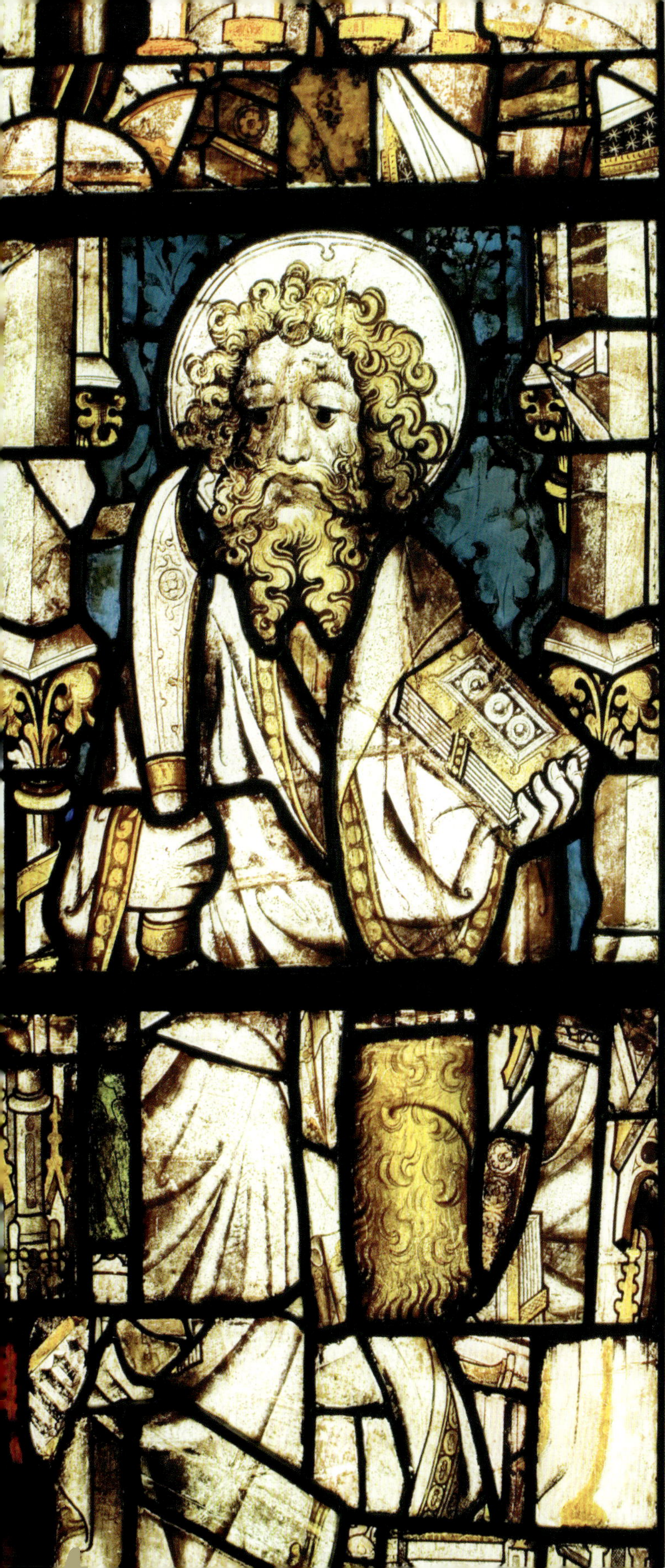

The monumental scale of this figure indicates its elevated setting, far above the ground. St Bartholomew was one of a series of prophets and apostles originally in the nave clerestory of Winchester Cathedral. Made between 1404 and 1422, the windows were funded by a bequest from Bishop William of Wykeham (died 1404), Chancellor of England and one of the most important patrons of medieval English stained glass. This panel was removed from the cathedral during the 'restoration' of 1852.

St Bartholomew, one of the apostles, was martyred by being flayed alive and is identified by the tanner's knife in his hand. Appropriately, he is the patron saint of shoemakers and bookbinders.

From Winchester Cathedral. On loan from the Victoria and Albert Museum, 2004.
(L2004.1)

MEDIEVAL STAINED GLASS OUTSIDE THE CHURCH AND CLOISTER

Although stained glass is most commonly associated with the cathedral, parish and monastic churches of the Middle Ages, by the end of the medieval period the houses of wealthier lay people were also sometimes glazed with stained glass. Diamond-shaped quarries and circular or oval roundels decorated with glass paint and silver stain were particularly popular, as their small-scale details could be appreciated in more intimate domestic settings. While some bespoke glazing schemes were made for the grandest houses and palaces, 'off-the-peg' panels were more common. Many of these were purchased in sets, for example, the 12 Labours of the Months, the Four Seasons, and the 12 Signs of the Zodiac. Other popular subjects included improving and moralising stories derived from both the Bible and vernacular allegorical sources.

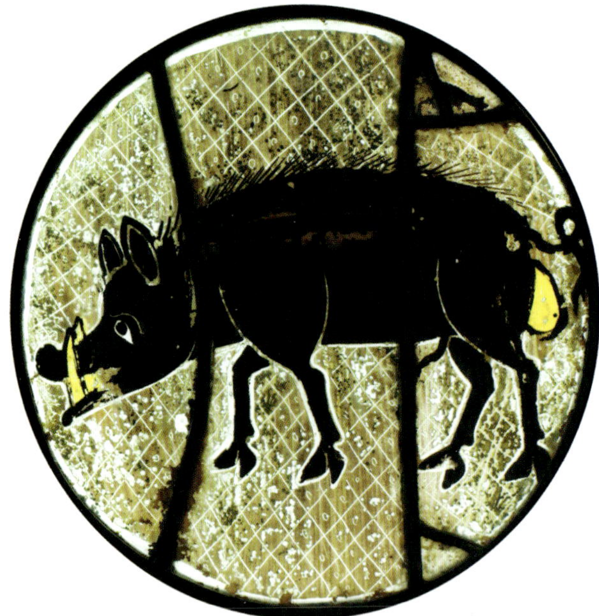

DE VERE ROUNDEL 14TH CENTURY
English artist

The wild boar was adopted by the de Vere family as a heraldic symbol because the Latin word *verres* means 'boar'. This roundel may have been made for John de Vere (1311–60), 7th Earl of Oxford, a trusted captain of Edward III in the king's wars in Scotland and France. The de Vere family seat was Castle Hedingham in Essex, but they held lands across England, particularly in East Anglia.

Original location in East Anglia, unknown.
On loan from the Norfolk and Norwich
Archaeological Society. (L2005.1)

OPPOSITE AND PAGE 5
ORDERS OF THE ANGELS:
THE VIRTUES AND THE PRINCIPALITIES
LATE 15TH CENTURY
English artist

The Orders of the Angels was a popular subject in medieval art and literature. As identified by the inscription *principans turma* ('ruling troop'), the Principalities were thought to govern the lands of kings, princes and bishops. Here they are shown wearing crowns and long, ermine-trimmed robes, typically associated with royalty, and hold palm branches. *Silver stain* is used to great effect in the wings, golden hair, crowns, and details on the robes, enlivening the whole image. The scale of these panels suggests they may have been made for a domestic setting.

Three angelic 'virtues' (see p. 5) are labelled with the Latin inscription *virtus uranica* ('heavenly virtues'), shown wearing diadems, dalmatic clerical robes and albs with apparels. They all hold open books, sceptres and, curiously, urine flasks. The inclusion of the urine flasks may be a pun on the word *uranica*, or perhaps indicates the virtues' power to perform healing miracles.

Original location in England, unknown.
Purchased with support from The Art Fund,
The ACE/V&A Purchase Grant Fund, 2015.
(2015.7.2 and 2015.7.1)

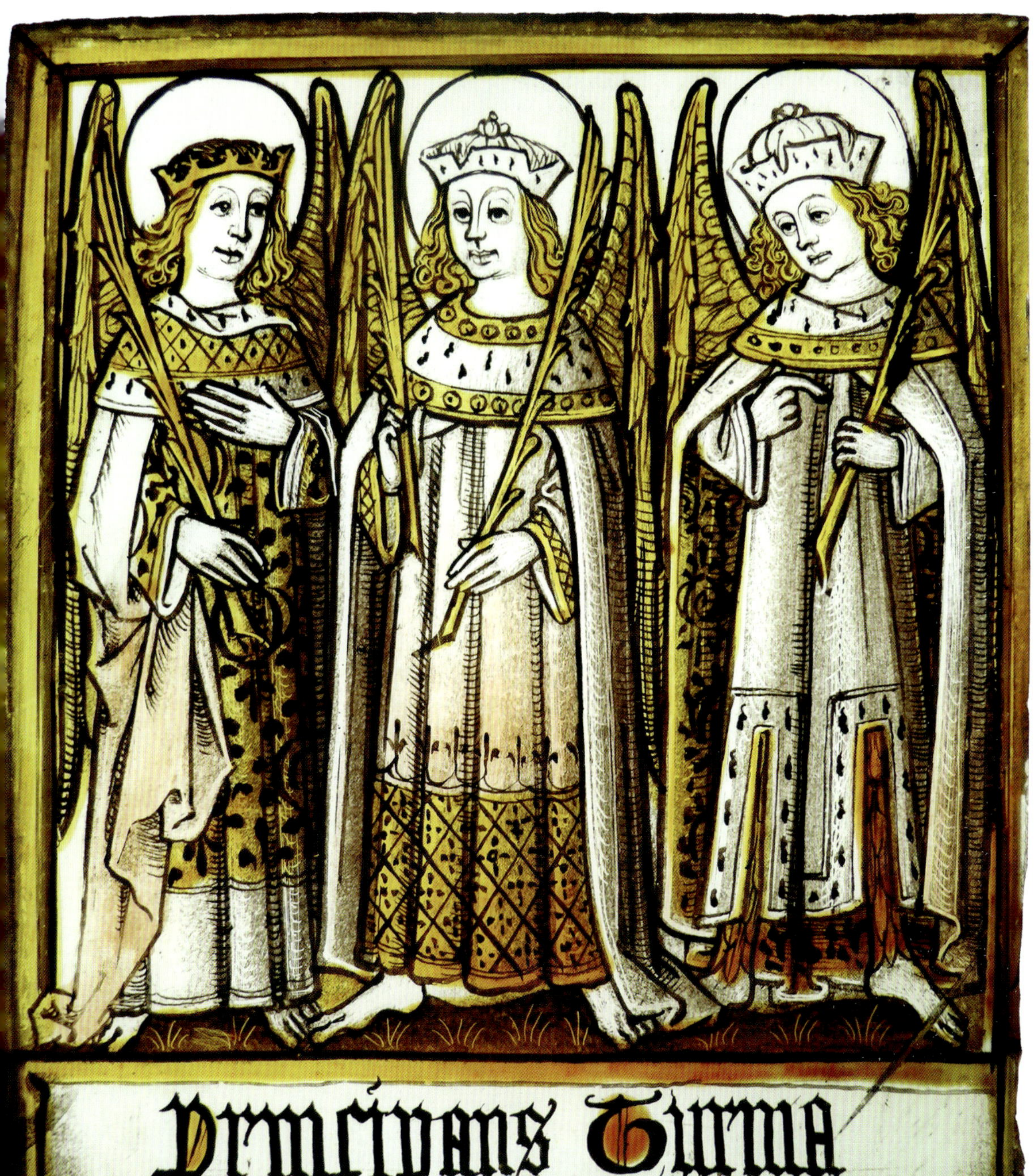
principans turma

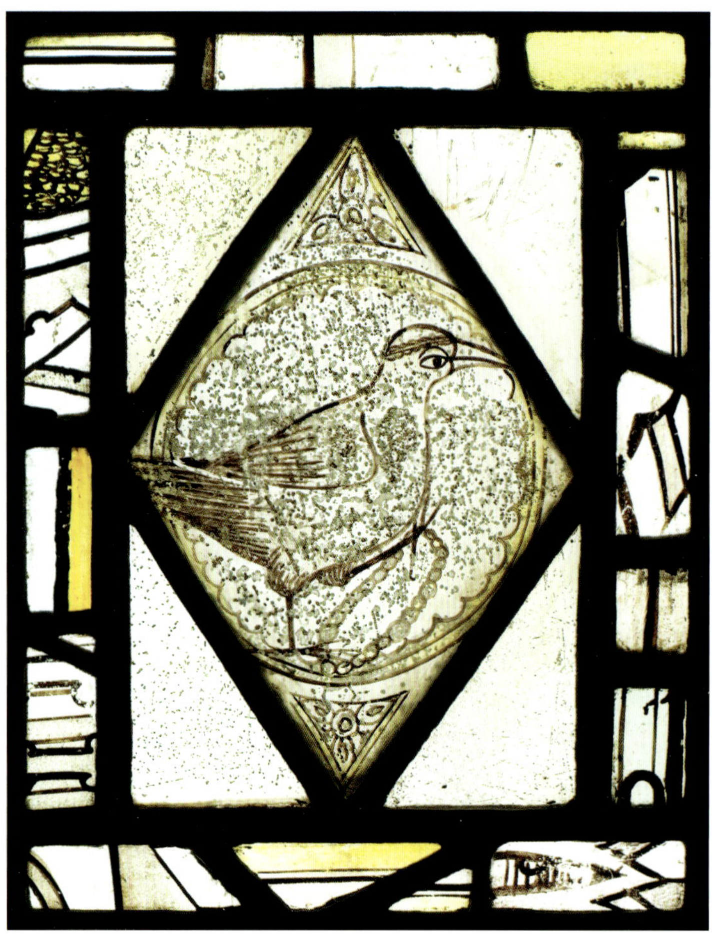

BIRD QUARRY 15TH CENTURY
English artist

Medieval quarries, often diamond-shaped, were the simplest form of stained glass, decorated using only glass paint and a little silver stain on clear or white glass. They were made in their thousands and often depicted flowers, or animals with amusing motifs that mocked human activities. This devout little bird is carrying a rosary. Other small medieval fragments have been incorporated into the border.

Original location in England, unknown. Purchased 1997. (1997.3)

REYNARD THE FOX
EARLY 15TH CENTURY
English artist

Here Reynard the Fox, a character from Aesop's *Fables*, is dressed as a monk or priest preaching to a flock of geese. The humorous depiction is a satire on the medieval clergy. Although highly valued for their exquisite painting, roundels were relatively inexpensive to produce, as they used only white or clear glass decorated with paint and silver stain. This panel exemplifies an irreverent strain found in much medieval art that coexisted alongside more conventional religious imagery.

Original location in England, unknown. On loan from the Rector and the Parochial Church Council of the Holy Cross, Byfield, Northamptonshire, 1990. (L1990.7.2)

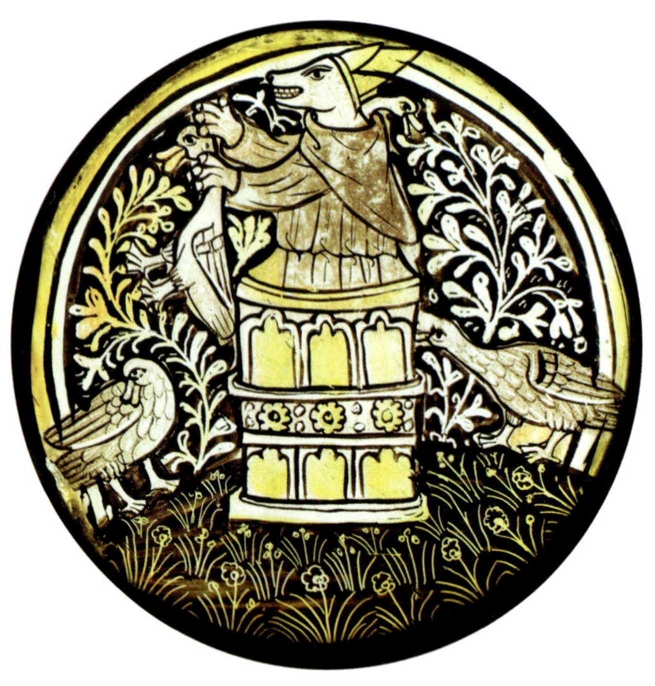

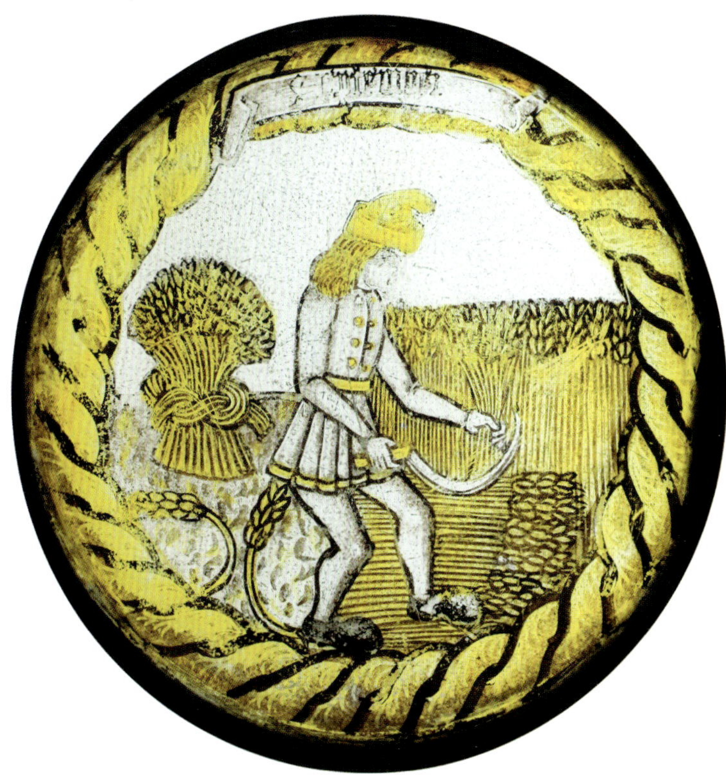

LABOURS OF THE MONTHS: SEPTEMBER, HARVESTING CORN; NOVEMBER, KILLING A BOAR

English artist

The Labours of the Month depicted familiar seasonal activities in the yearly cycle of agricultural life. A favourite subject for stained glass roundels set into windows in domestic settings, they were often bought in sets. Each of these scenes has a twisted rope border. In 'September' a labourer with a sickle prepares to cut a handful of corn to join the pile at his feet. Behind him a standing sheaf of corn has been bound with plaited stalks. In 'November' a labourer brandishing an axe turns to face a boar on the right, the knife and bowl to his left ready to collect its blood. In medieval calendars the fattening up and slaughtering of pigs was a popular image for the months of November and December.

From Matfield House, Kent. On loan from the Victoria and Albert Museum, 2004.
(L2004.6 and L2004.7)

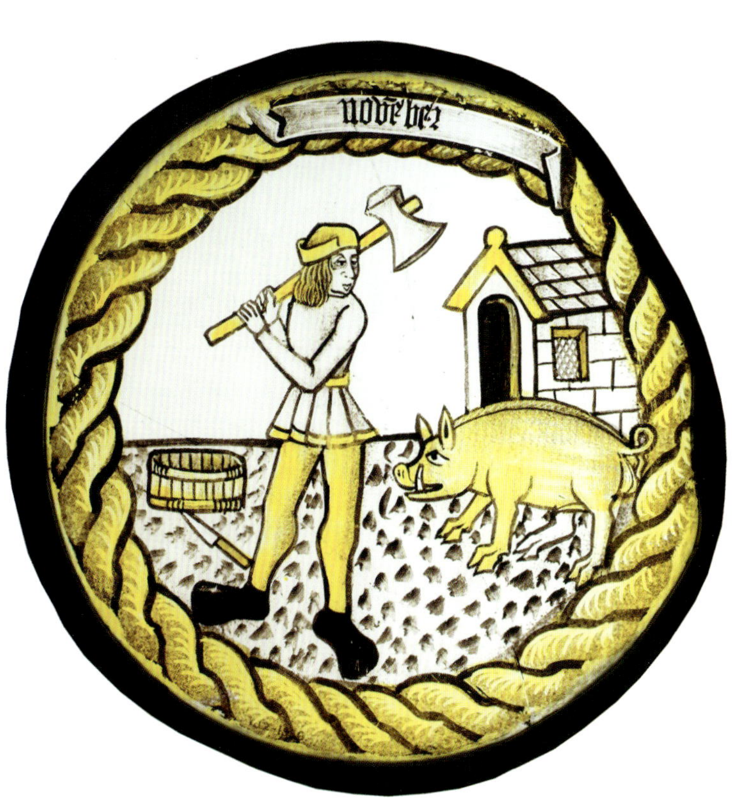

NORFOLK IN THE 15TH CENTURY

By the late 15th century the wool trade had made Norwich the richest and largest city outside London. With a cathedral and over fifty parish churches (of which 31 remain), it became a major centre for the production of stained glass, supplying windows not only for its own churches but also for many sites in East Anglia. Glass painters were among the city's richest citizens, filling many of the highest offices in its government, another measure of the social standing of the craft. Many stained glass windows were lost as a result of destruction at the Reformation in the 16th century and in the years following the English Civil War, when Protestant Reformers, notably the zealous William Dowsing, were entrusted with the task of erasing 'superstitious' religious images. Nonetheless, a sufficient quantity of stained glass made by 15th- and early 16th-century Norwich glass painters has survived to demonstrate the lively character of their painting style and their extraordinary levels of skill. Their work constitutes a distinctive and important East Anglian contribution to the art of late medieval England, illustrated here in a series of panels on loan from the Victoria and Albert Museum.

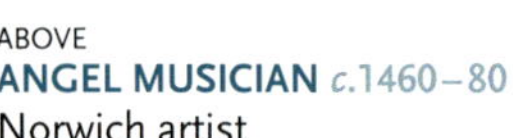

ANGEL MUSICIAN *c.*1460–80
Norwich artist

Angels were very common in Norfolk churches, in both the timber roofs and in the *tracery* openings of stained glass windows. Musical angels often accompanied scenes such as the Annunciation to the Virgin Mary or her Coronation by Christ as the Queen of Heaven. This angel, its feathered attire possibly inspired by costumes in medieval drama, plays a vielle, a stringed instrument. The vigorous linear drawing and the so-called 'ears of barley' motif on the pedestal at the angel's feet suggest that this panel was probably made in a workshop previously run by John Wighton, a dignitary on the town council.

Original location in England, unknown. On loan from the Victoria and Albert Museum, 2004. (L2004.3)

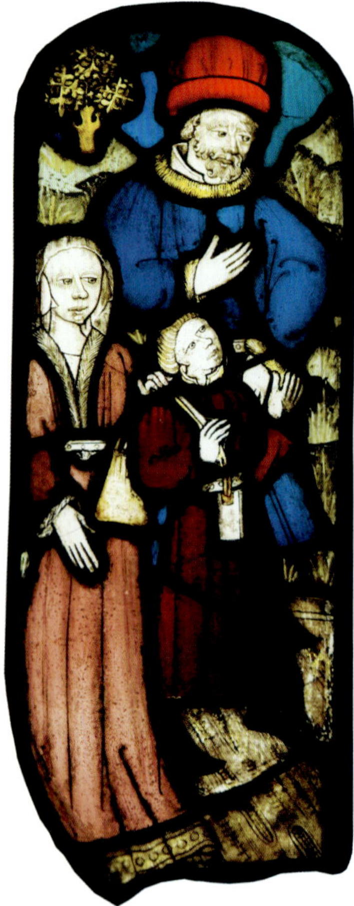

RIGHT
SCENE FROM THE LIFE OF ST BENEDICT *c.*1460–80
Norwich artist

This panel, from the same Norwich workshop as the musical angel, depicts St Benedict as a boy being sent off to school by his parents. Over his shoulder he carries a bag and dangling from its strap is a hornbook, from which children learned the alphabet: letters were inscribed on a piece of parchment backed with wood and covered with a transparent layer of animal horn. The image closely resembles another in the Bedford Breviary, a 15th-century manuscript belonging to the Duke of Bedford.

Original location in England, unknown. On loan from the Victoria and Albert Museum, 2004. (L2004.5)

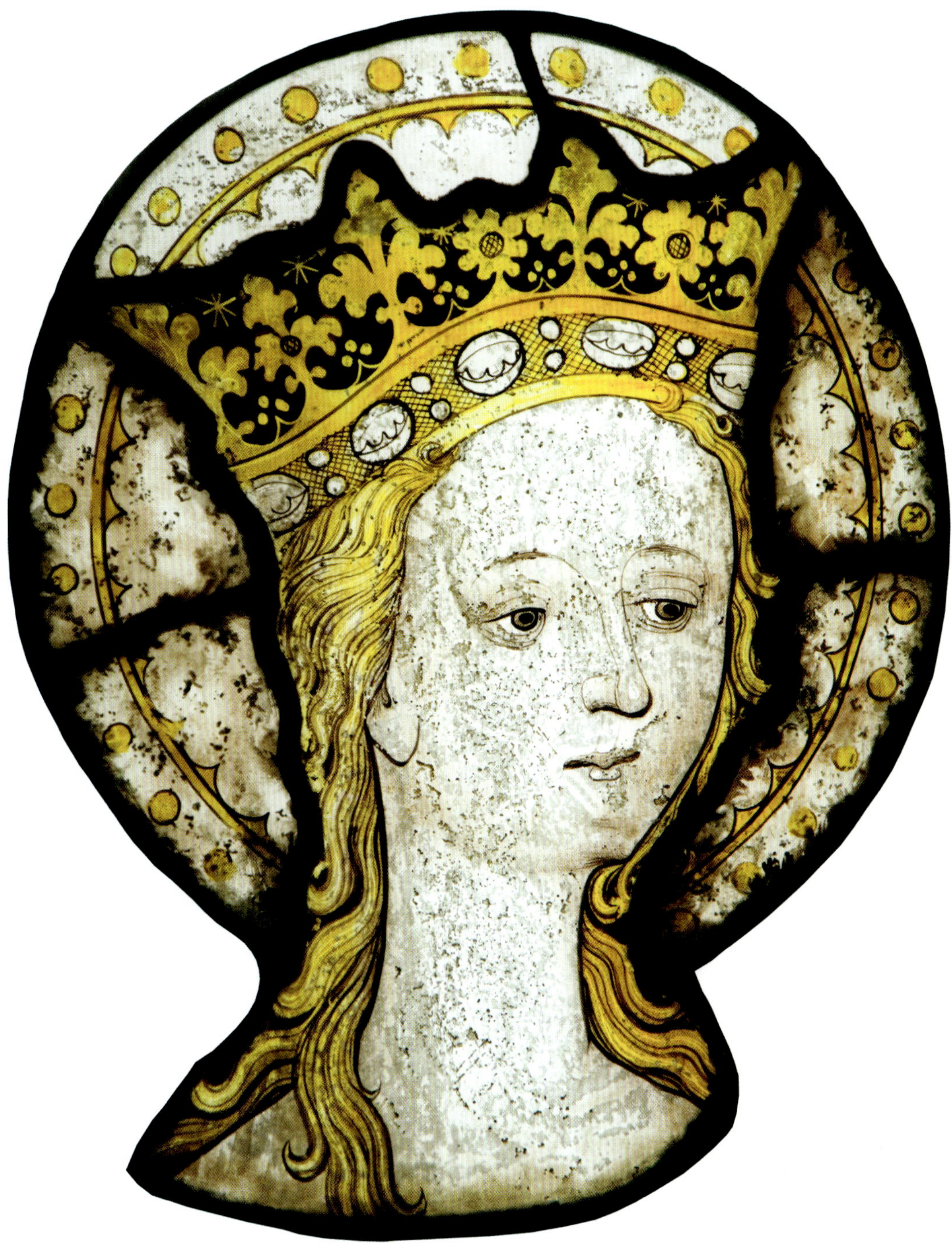

CROWNED FEMALE HEAD *c.*1440–60
Norwich artist

This female, with long blonde hair, wears an ornate crown on her head. She may be the Virgin Mary, depicted as the Queen of Heaven: Mary was by far the most prevalent female image during the Middle Ages, but other female saints were also sometimes shown crowned. The fine painting style suggests it was made in Norwich around the middle of the 15th century.

Original location in England unknown. On loan from the Victoria and Albert Museum, 2004. (L2004.4)

GLASS PAINTING IN THE 16th CENTURY

Some of the most spectacular stained glass windows of this period were produced in the Low Countries (modern-day Belgium and the Netherlands). These artists made great use of new materials, including striated and flashed glass and a new red pigment, sanguine. Pioneering artists introduced a more realistic style to their glass painting, which mirrored developments in panel painting. Through trade and political contacts with the Continent, English patrons became aware of these advances. In the closing decades of the 15th century many European artists migrated to England, much to the dismay of the native craft guilds. In 1497 a Flemish artist, Barnard Flower, was appointed glass painter to Henry VII. Thereafter the choicest commissions were entrusted to workshops led by foreign glass painters. The famous stained glass windows at Fairford Church, Gloucestershire; St George's Chapel, Windsor; Henry VII's Chapel at Westminster Abbey; and King's College Chapel, Cambridge, can all be attributed to these Anglo-Netherlandish artist craftsmen.

The dramatic religious upheaval of the Reformation was experienced across many European countries. In England, Henry VIII's break with Rome led to the destruction of shrines, the dissolution of the monasteries and extensive damage to hundreds of great churches and their contents, cutting short the renaissance of stained glass. However, in the 19th century the glass painting styles of 16th-century European artists remained popular with collectors, who took advantage of the upheavals of the French Revolution and Napoleonic Wars to import their work into England in considerable quantities. The Museum has two major examples of early 16th-century continental stained glass, evidence of the inventive design and technical virtuosity that so appealed to English patrons in the reigns of Henry VII and Henry VIII.

THE SUICIDE OF CHARONDAS OF CATANEA *c.1530*
Attributed to Dirick Vellert (*c.*1480–1547)

The story of Charondas of Catanea, who broke his own laws and killed himself, was used by Roman author Valerius Maximus to illustrate concepts of Justice. Allegorical stories and episodes from classical history were popular with educated patrons of the 16th century in the Low Countries. Thousands of such roundels were produced in Belgium and the Netherlands in the 16th and 17th centuries, and were prized more for their skilful execution than for the value of the materials from which they were made. Their small size and exquisite detail made them popular with English collectors of the late 18th and 19th centuries. Dirick Vellert, who may have designed this example, was one of Antwerp's foremost glass designers.

Original location unknown. From the collection of Thomas Cowell. Donated by John Wilson, 1992. (1992.4.12)

SCENE FROM THE LEGEND OF ST JAMES *c.*1500–50
French artist

This scene may depict the trial of a pilgrim, from the legend of St James the Great. The whereabouts of other panels from the window are unknown; this small section displays the extraordinary technical virtuosity of 16th-century glass painters. The red and blue hats of the soldiers on the right are made of flashed glass, abraded and stained. Small amounts of sanguine have been used to create flesh tones and red lips. The painting style suggests that the panel may have come from Normandy, perhaps Rouen, where glass painting had been reinvigorated by the Netherlandish artist Arnold of Nijmegen.

Original location in France, probably Rouen. From the collection of Dr William Cole. Purchased with assistance from The Art Fund and The Beecroft Foundation, 1998. (1998.4)

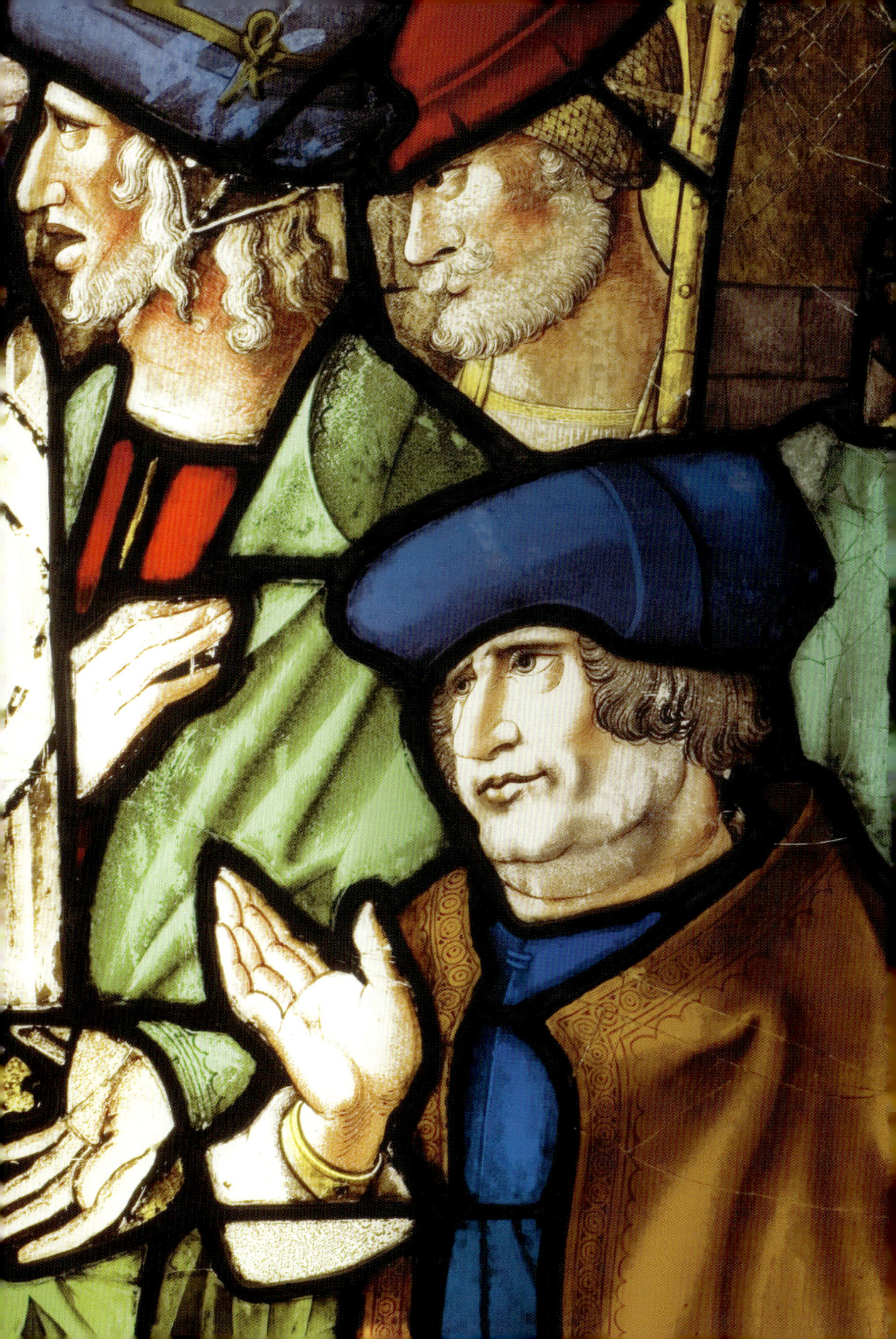

THE AGE OF ENAMELS 1640–1830

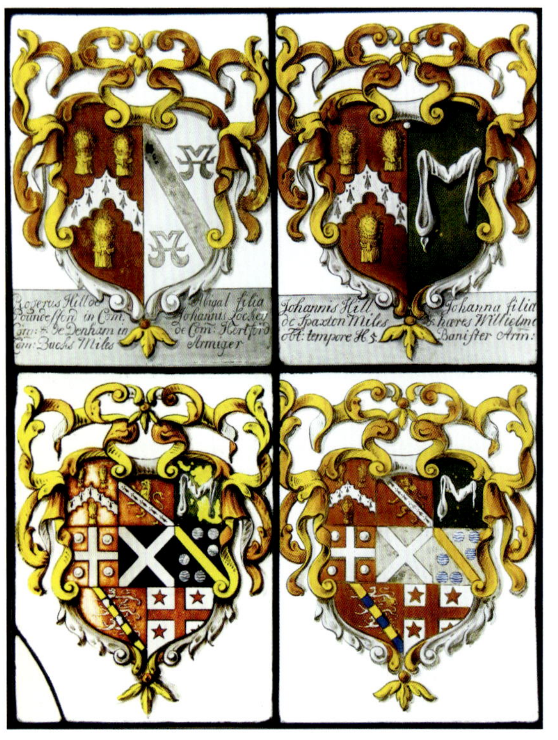

Following the Reformation the demand for new stained glass windows declined considerably, as did the supply of pot metal glass, although heraldic glass remained popular, especially in country houses. During the reigns of James I and Charles I a more tolerant attitude to religious stained glass prevailed, particularly under Archbishop of Canterbury William Laud. But this 'Laudian Revival' was short-lived and the outbreak of the Civil War in 1642 brought another period of destruction. During the Commonwealth bishoprics were abolished and some of England's eastern counties experienced campaigns of officially mandated iconoclasm.

By the time the monarchy was restored in 1660, the Gothic style was replaced by a growing range of translucent enamel colours that could be painted and fired directly onto clear glass. This innovation meant it was no longer necessary to spend time cutting pieces of coloured glass to form a design, and in the 17th and 18th centuries stained glass became much closer to oil painting in its technique, approach and even its appearance. Indeed, English glass paintings of this period often copied oil paintings by famous artists. Arguably much of the finest enamel-painted glass was produced in the Netherlands, Germany and Switzerland. The techniques were ideally suited to the complexities of small-scale domestic panels.

SHIELDS OF ARMS *c.*1691–95
Possibly by William Price the Elder (died 1709)

Heraldry, rather than figurative work, remained a popular form of stained glass throughout the 17th and 18th centuries. These panels depict the arms of the Hill family of Denham Place and come from a large window in the family chapel demonstrating the family's lineage. They were originally made for Sir Roger Hill, to demonstrate his family's lineage, but these panels were later relocated to the family chapel and supplemented with additional shields of the Way family, who inherited the estate from the Hill family through marriage. Some of the coloured enamel pigment has been lost over time.

From the Chapel, Denham Place, Buckinghamshire. On loan from Denham Place, 1979. (L1979.4.2–5)

COMMEMORATIVE PANEL 1646
Attributed to Jakob Weber I (1610–58)

Jakob Weber father and son worked in Winterthur, Switzerland, during the 17th century, where the popularity of secular panels commemorating marriages, battles and other events countered to some extent the decline in demand for religious stained glass following the Reformation. Here Frederick Hans Sturtzenegger, shown as a standard bearer in full armour, is offered a goblet by his wife. In the background a castle is under siege. The panel may commemorate Sturtzenegger's role in protecting the city.

Original location unknown, Switzerland. On loan from the Victoria and Albert Museum, 1984. (L1984.3.1)

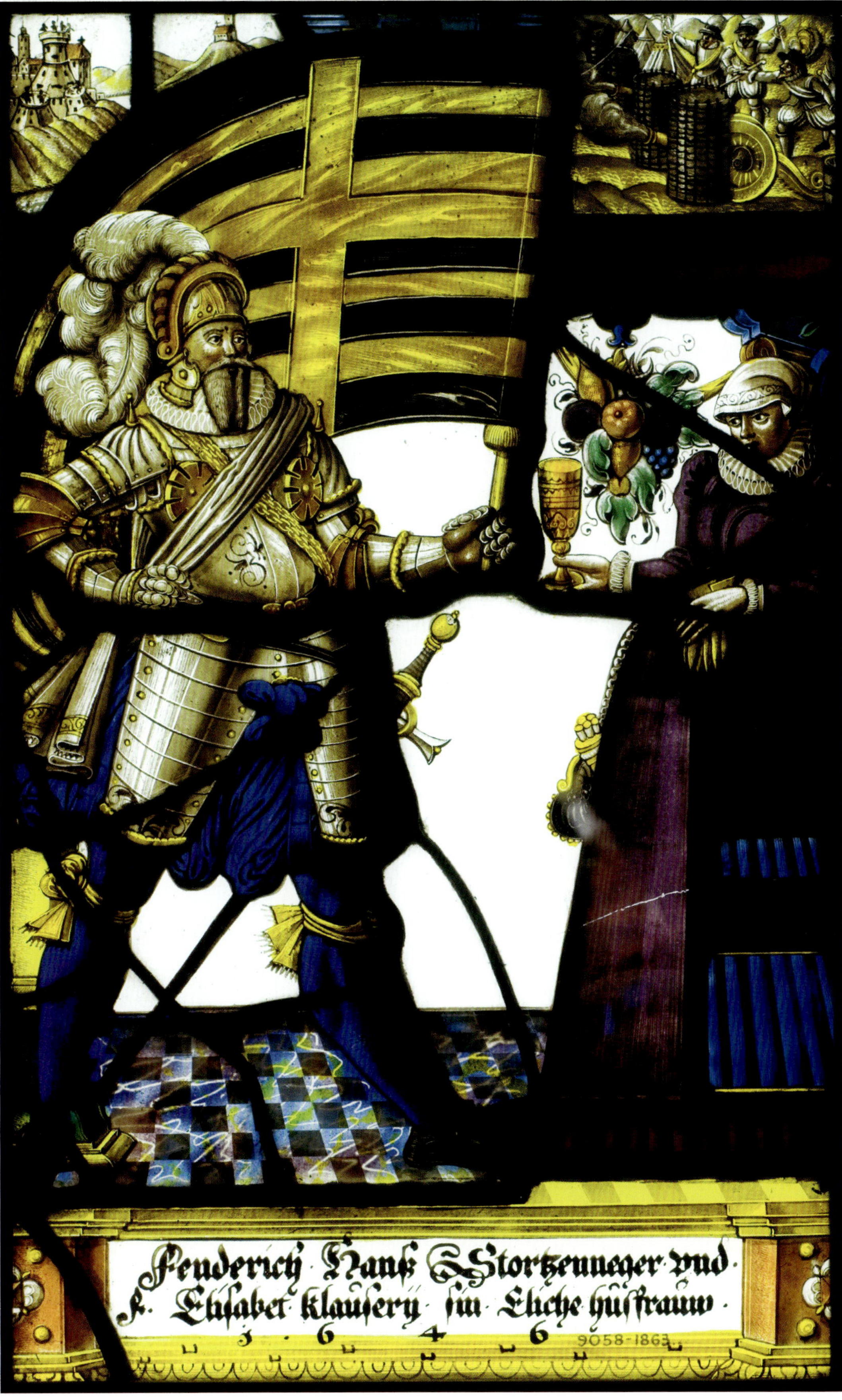

Fenderich Hanß Storßenneger vnd
F. Elisabet klauseri sin Eliche huszfrauw
1 6 4 6
9058-1863

NICHOLAS RIDLEY, *c.*1650 AND 1800
English artist

Bishop of London Nicholas Ridley was a leading Protestant reformer during the reign of Edward VI (1547–53). Imprisoned by Queen Mary and declared a heretic, he was burnt at the stake in Oxford in 1555 with fellow reformer Bishop Hugh Latimer. This 17th-century enamel-painted portrait has been enlarged by the addition of an 18th-century surround. It is thought to have come from Leez Priory in Essex, which upon its suppression by Henry VIII was acquired by Richard, 1st Baron Rich.

Probably from Leez Priory, Essex. Purchased 1995. (1979.1)

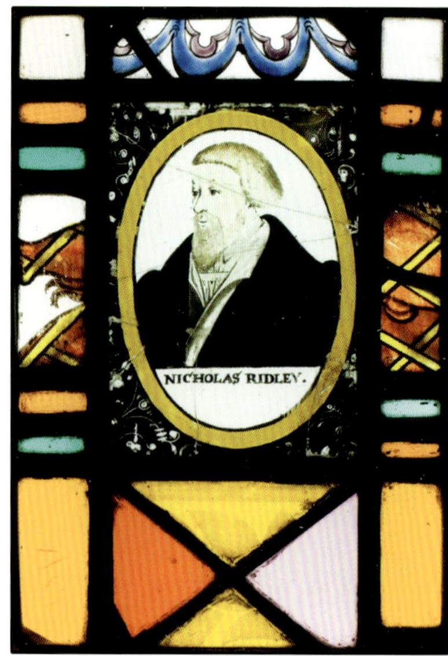

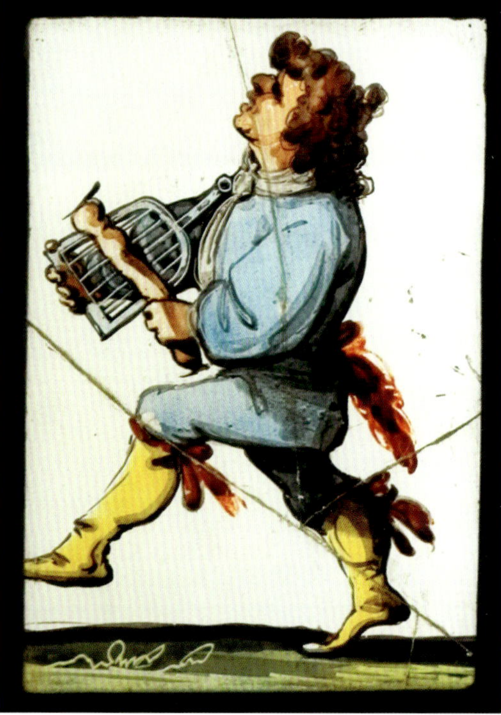

MUSICIAN FROM THE NEAVE COLLECTION
17TH CENTURY
Dutch artist

Sir Thomas Neave of Dagnam Park, Essex, had a fine collection of stained glass, much of which he purchased from importer and dealer John Christopher Hampp of Norwich. Several small panels featuring musicians playing instruments including the bagpipes, drum, violin, lute, cello and hurdy-gurdy, may have been installed as 'cabinet pieces' in Neave's home. Among the caricatures is an unusual musician – a butcher playing a griddle with a sausage!

Original location unknown. From the Neave Collection. On loan from David King, 2009. (L2009.9)

DOG SEATED ON A CUSHION 1756
Made by William Peckitt (baptised 1731, died 1795)

This 18th-century pet portrait shows a lapdog sitting on a red cushion, framed by a rococo border. It came from Gisburne Park, an 18th-century country house in Lancashire owned by Thomas Lister, who ordered the panel from William Peckitt of York in March 1756. Peckitt was the most significant glass painter of his time, known across the country for his skilled enamel painting. He painted another version of this subject for the daughter of John Bourchier of Benningborough Hall, Yorkshire.

From Gisburne Park, Lancashire. Purchased 2010. (2010.3.1)

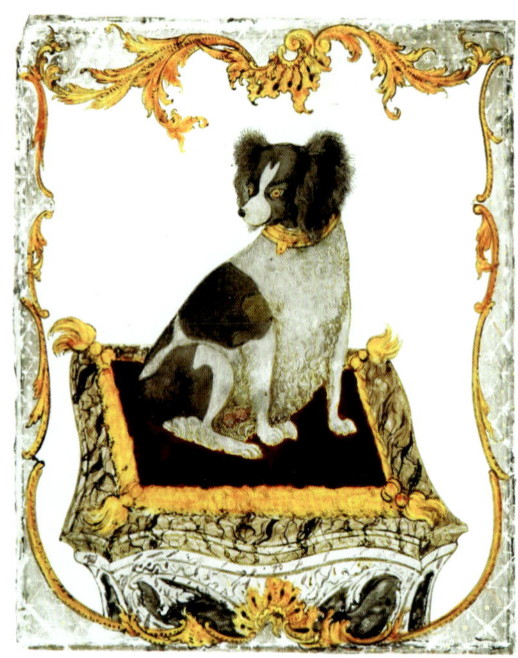

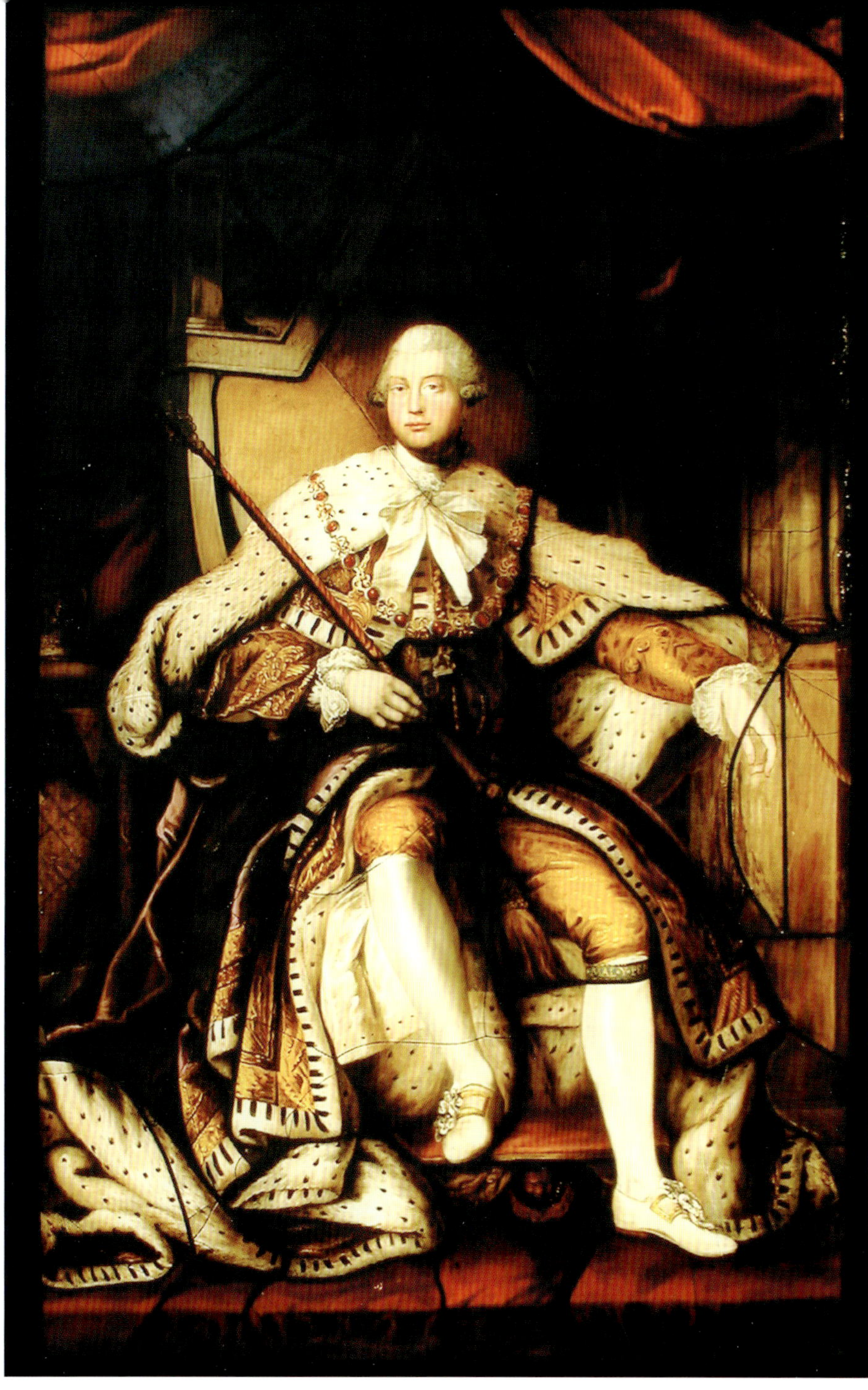

PORTRAIT OF GEORGE III 1793
Made by James Pearson (*c.*1740–1838) after a painting by Sir Joshua Reynolds (1723–92)

This monumental image of George III in ceremonial robes, seated on the medieval coronation chair in Westminster Abbey, is a copy on glass of Sir Joshua Reynolds's Coronation portrait of 1780. Painted almost entirely using coloured enamel pigments on white glass, the window demonstrates the skill of James Pearson and his wife, Margaret Eglington, using large pieces of glass so that the leads could be hidden in the design. Pearson cleverly concealed an iron frame behind the painted glass to give it extra structural support.

Lent by Her Majesty the Queen, 1992. (L1992.6)

SHIELDS OF ARMS 1829

Designed by David Evans (1793–1861); made by Betton
& Evans

These shields, which originally accompanied the Four
Evangelists, commemorate the Le Strange, Bassett de
Blore and Stanley families, all of whom had connections
to Ellesmere and its church. The bright colours are
typical of the glass available to glass painters before the
revival of so-called antique glasses in the later 1840s.

From the Church of St Mary, Ellesmere, Shropshire.
Donated by the Diocese of Lichfield, 2014. (1975.6)

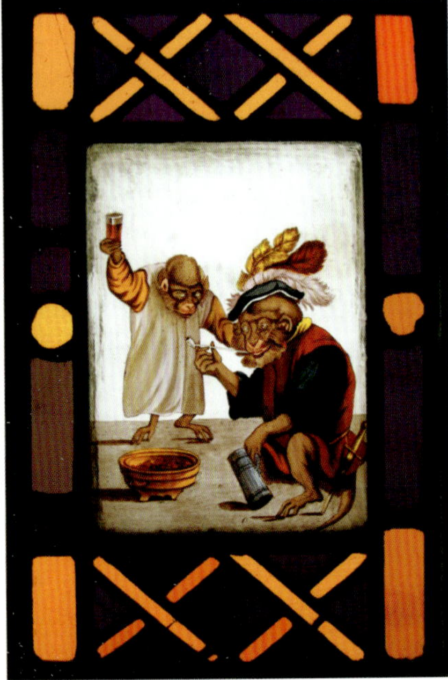

MONKEYS DRINKING AND SMOKING, FROM A SERIES OF VICES *c.*1800–15
English artist

Monkeys drinking, smoking, gambling and
playing musical instruments were commonly
used to illustrate human vices and mock society
in the 17th century. This panel is one of a series
based on the 17th-century paintings of David
Teniers the Younger, who lived in Antwerp and
later in Brussels. This panel and its companions
may have been copied from engravings of his
paintings, which were widely circulated.

Original location unknown.
Bequest of Miss M.S. Rickard, 2008. (2008.5.6)

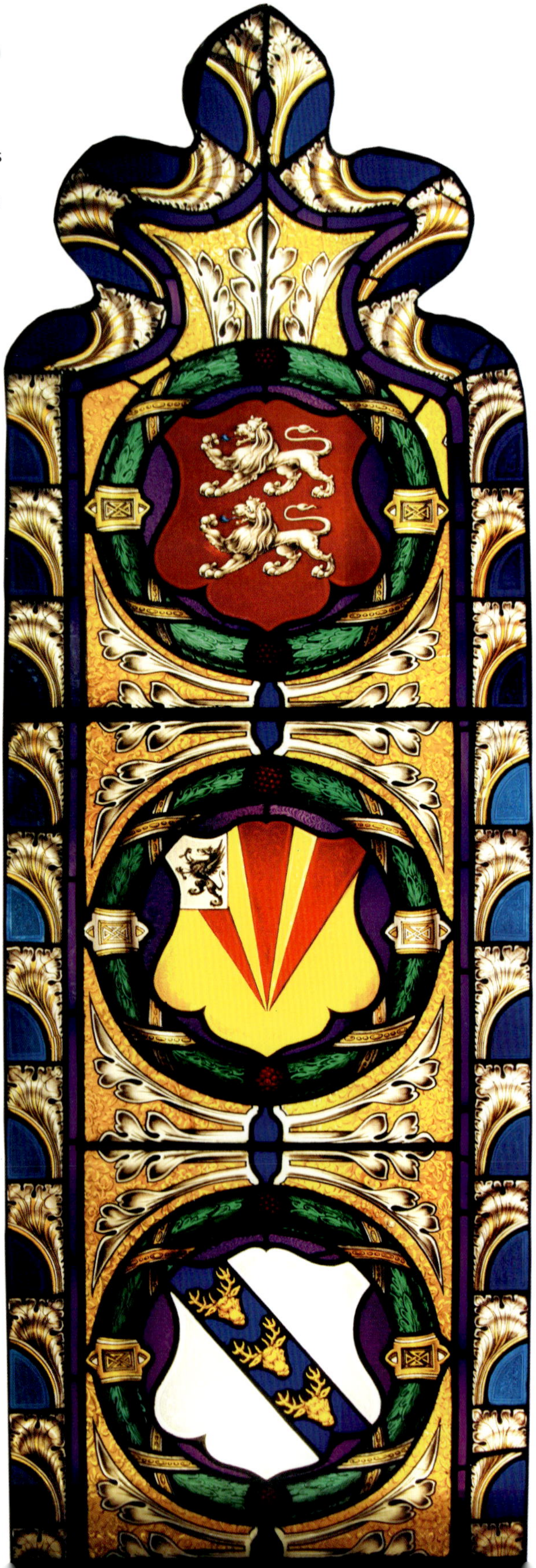

Attributed to a student of William Collins (1773–1845)

This fine example of enamel painting on glass is copied from a *cartoon* for a tapestry by Raphael now in the Victoria and Albert Museum. A stained glass panel of the same subject, signed by London glass painter William Collins, can also be seen in the collection of the Victoria and Albert Museum. The version in the Stained Glass Museum's collection is unsigned and may have been made by one of Collins's students.

Original location unknown. Purchased 1996. (1996.2)

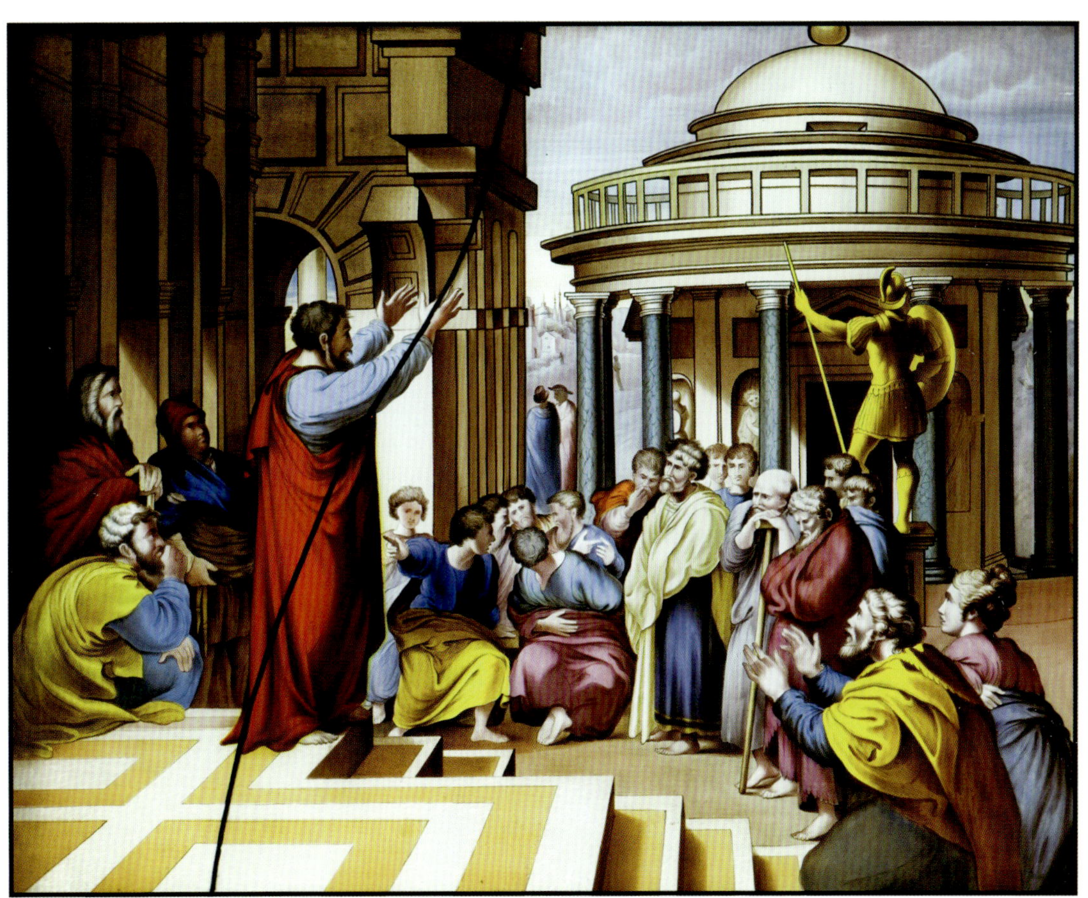

RECOVERING 'TRUE PRINCIPLES'

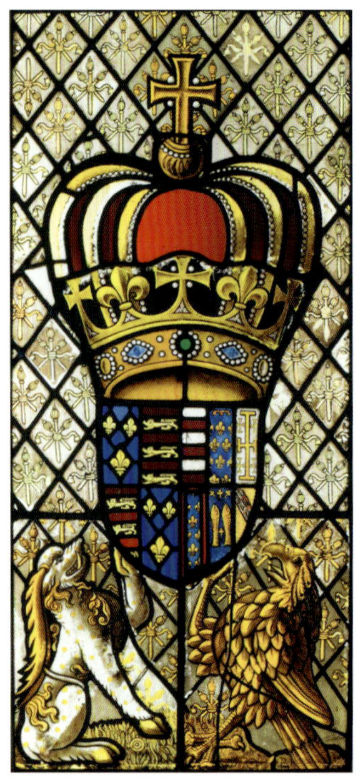

Although stained glass declined in popularity after the Reformation, circumstances in the early 1800s favoured a revival. Parliamentary building acts granted the Church of England the extraordinary sum of £1,500,000 to build new churches for the growing population; Catholic Emancipation from 1829 enabled Roman Catholics to worship freely, boosting demand for new Catholic churches; and Nonconformist congregations built new churches, chapels and meeting houses. Churches were built in a variety of different architectural styles, but the far-reaching Gothic Revival gained ground. 'Pictorial' enamel-painted glass soon gave way to a flatter, more two-dimensional approach with the rediscovery of medieval stained glass techniques.

The pioneering architect and designer A.W.N. Pugin played a key role in reviving the art in Britain. He advocated a return to 'True Principles' and worked with several glass painters to recreate the Gothic style, including Thomas Willement, William Wailes, William Warrington and John Hardman, all of whose work is represented in the Museum's collection. The restoration of medieval glazing schemes gave stained glass artists first-hand experience of ancient glass, and a number of publications gave craftsmen and designers invaluable information about historic stained glass. Among the most important were those by Charles Winston, a patent lawyer and amateur historian of stained glass, who became aware of the relatively poor quality of the glass available to artists of his own day, which was often thin and garish in colour. In 1857 he encouraged experiments to rediscover the chemical components of medieval glass and, with Dr Medlock, a chemist, persuaded Edward Green at the London firm of James Powell & Sons to make antique glass to his recipes. By the 1860s, thanks to renewed appreciation and knowledge of medieval stained glass and developments in glassmaking, artists were able to design and make stained glass windows that rivalled their historic counterparts in design, tone and quality of glass.

ABOVE
THE ARMS OF QUEEN MARGARET OF ANJOU *c.*1840
Attributed to Thomas Willement (1786–1871)

These heraldic arms, supported by an eagle and a heraldic antelope, were faithfully copied from a 15th-century armorial window in the Great Hall at Ockwells Manor in Berkshire. This window was probably made by heraldic scholar, designer and stained glass artist Thomas Willement. Often referred to as 'the Father of Victorian Stained Glass', Willement was Heraldic Artist to George IV and Artist in Stained Glass to Queen Victoria; he trained several other important designers and makers of stained glass.

From the church of Holy Trinity, Crockerton Wiltshire. Donated by the Church Commissioners, 1974. (1974.3.1b)

OPPOSITE, DETAIL
NOLI ME TANGERE (DO NOT TOUCH ME) 1852
Designed by John Hardman Powell (1832–95); made by John Hardman & Co.

This panel is part of an east window illustrating the Betrayal, Crucifixion and the Resurrection of Christ. In 1845 A.W.N. Pugin persuaded his friend and fellow Roman Catholic John Hardman to expand his ecclesiastical metalworks to include stained glass manufacture. In Hardman & Co. Pugin had at last found a studio that satisfied his exacting standards. Their joint display in the Medieval Court of the Great Exhibition of 1851, with other collaborators, was highly influential in the development of the Gothic Revival.

From the chapel of St James, Clifton, Oxford. Donated by the Diocese of Oxford, 1975. (1975.5.7)

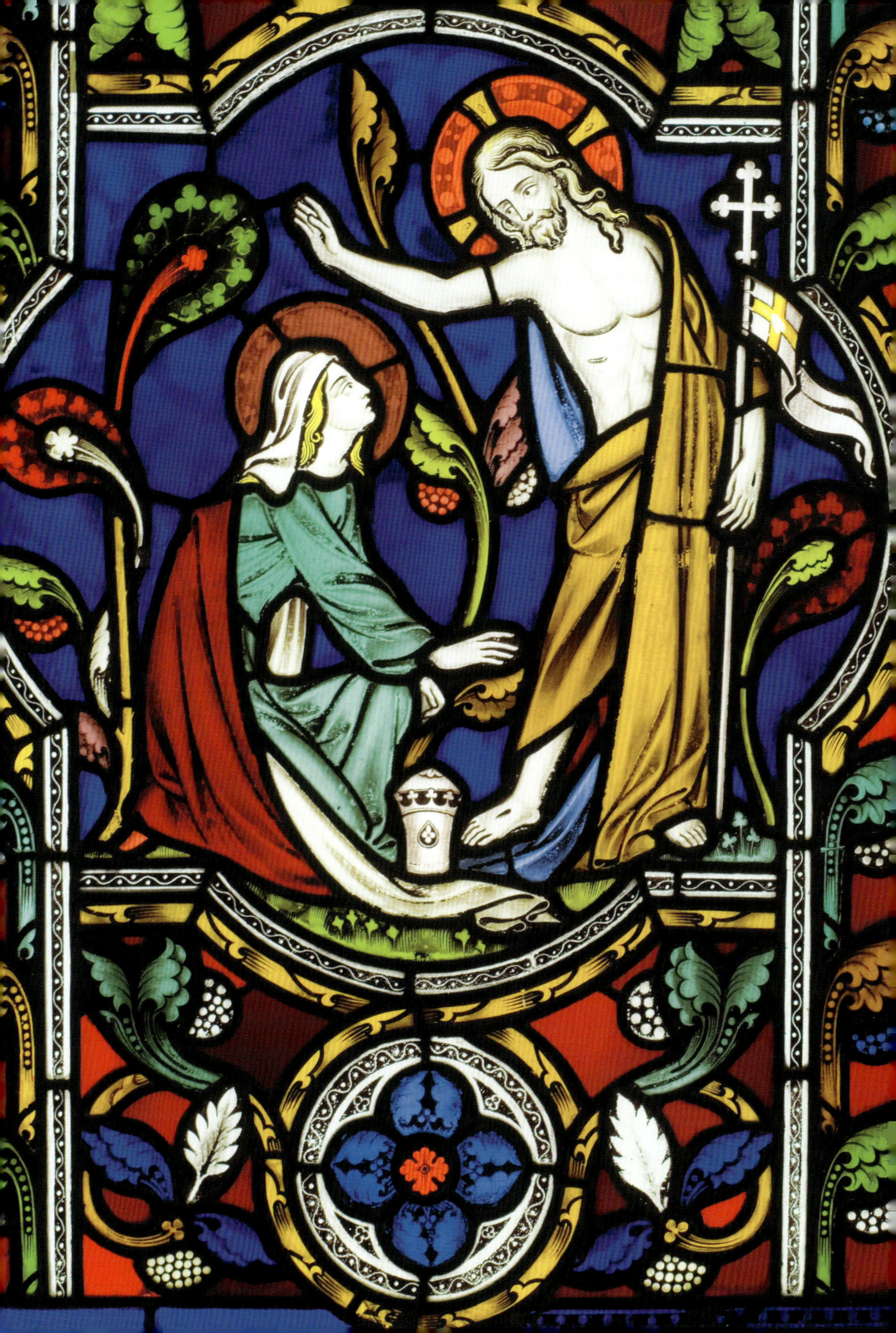

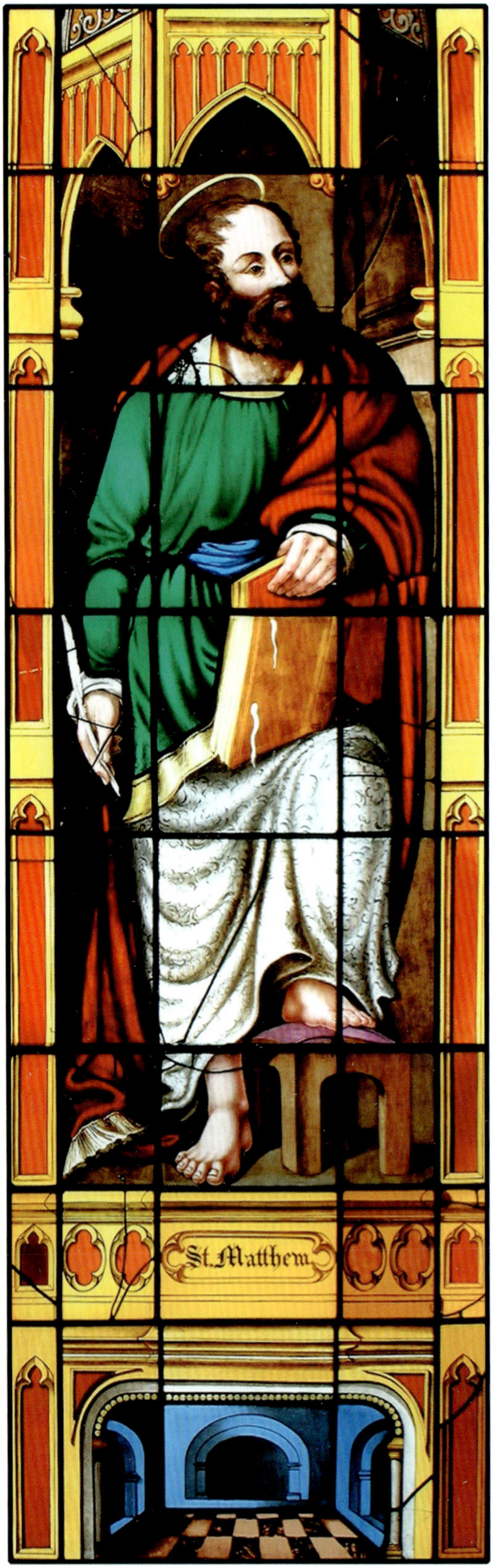

LEFT
ST MATTHEW *c.*1830
Attributed to Thomas Wright of Leeds
(active from 1775)

This window demonstrates how the
18th-century technique of painting in
enamel pigments on large rectangles of
white glass continued well into the 19th
century. The panel was created using a
combination of both enamel-painted and
pot metal coloured glass. The placement
of the figure of St Matthew under a
Gothic-style architectural canopy reveals
the impact of the early Gothic Revival.

*From the church of St Matthew, Holbeck,
Yorkshire. Donated by the Ripon Diocesan
Board of Finance, 1981.* (1981.5)

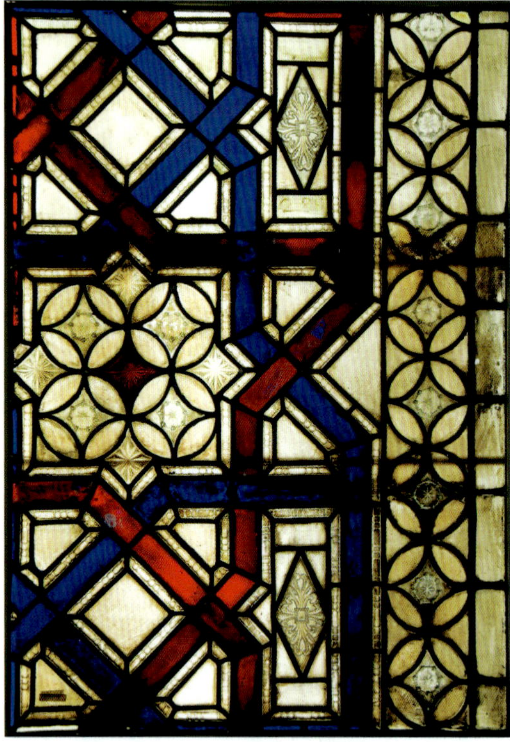

ABOVE
STAMPED QUARRIES 1849
Made by James Powell & Sons

This unusual panel demonstrates how industrial
manufacturing processes influenced stained glass
manufacture. These moulded and textured quarries were
created by stamping, rolling and pressing soft glass into
indented moulds. The process enabled Powell & Sons
to offer clients across the world a cheaper and effective
form of glazing. The indented patterns were sometimes
also decorated with glass paint and silver stain and fired
in the usual manner.

*From the church of St Thomas, Kingly Street, London W1.
Donated by the Church Commissioners, 1973.* (1973.1)

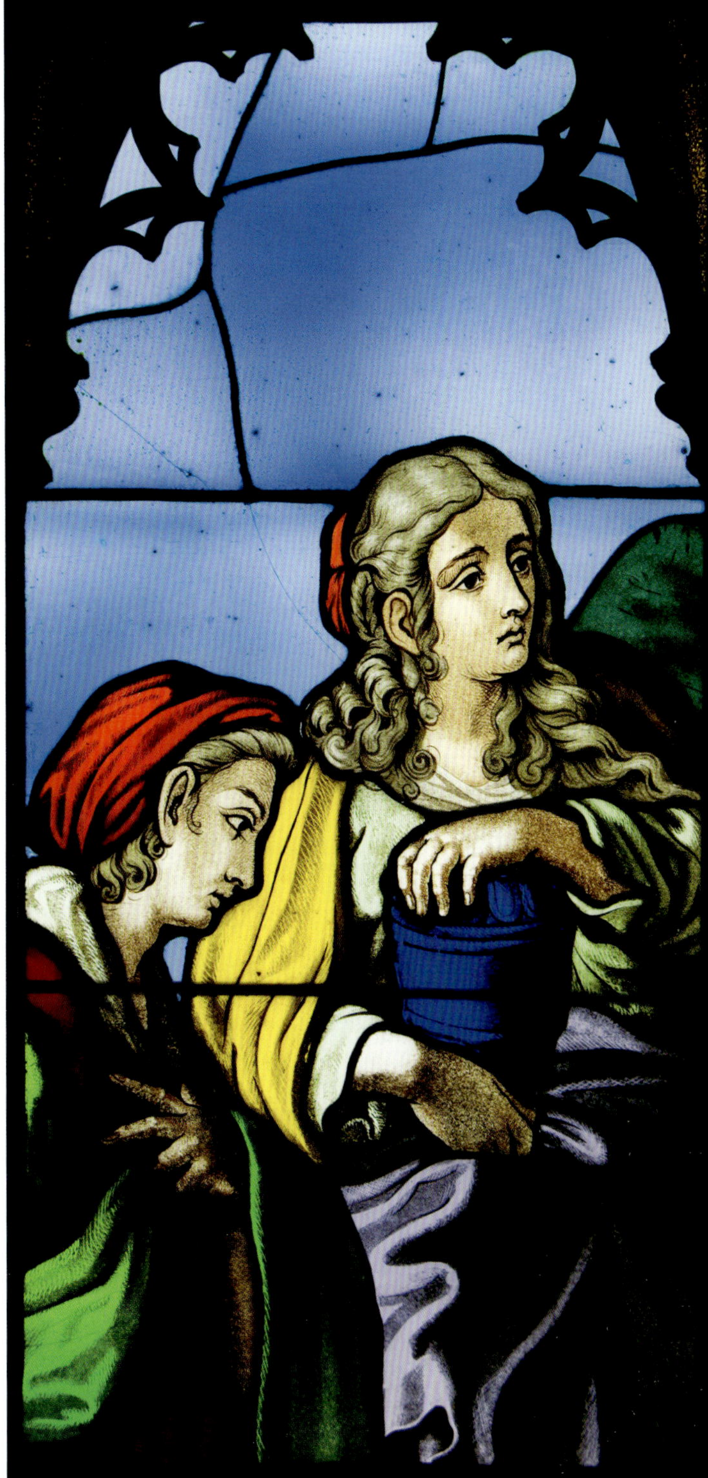

THE MARYS AT THE TOMB 1856
Designed and made by George
Hedgeland (active *c.*1850–59)

Hedgeland's career in stained glass
was short but distinguished. He
exhibited at the Great Exhibition of
1851, and in 1854 was commissioned
to make the great west window of
Norwich Cathedral, one of his finest
creations. In 1860, in poor health,
he sold his studio and emigrated to
Australia, where he died. His work is
characterised by large pieces of richly
coloured glass, softly painted with
delicate cross-hatching reminiscent
of 16th-century paintings. By the
end of the 19th century his broad,
pictorial style had fallen from favour.
In this detail from a large window,
Mary, the wife of Cleophas, and Mary
Magdalene, carrying a blue jar of
spices, arrive to see the empty tomb
of Christ after his resurrection.

*From the church of St Mary, Great
Brington, Northamptonshire. On loan
from the Rector and Parochial Church
Council of St Mary's, Great Brington,
1975.* (L1975.2.2b)

CHRIST BLESSING THE CHILDREN 1856

Designed and made by Thomas
Wilmshurst (1806–80) after a design
by Friedrich Overbeck (1789–1869)

Originally located in St Catherine's
Chapel, then in use as a baptistery
chapel, this window is based on a
painting by Friedrich Overbeck,
a founding member of the German
Romantic brotherhood of artists
called the Nazarenes. Wilmshurst
was influenced by the tranquil, rather
sombre style of Overbeck's work.
The window was replaced in the 1930s
with a window of the Crucifixion by
Hugh Easton (1906–65).

*From St Catherine's Chapel, Ely Cathedral.
On loan from the Dean and Chapter of
Ely Cathedral, 1980. Conservation funded
by The Worshipful Company of Glaziers.*
(L1989.4)

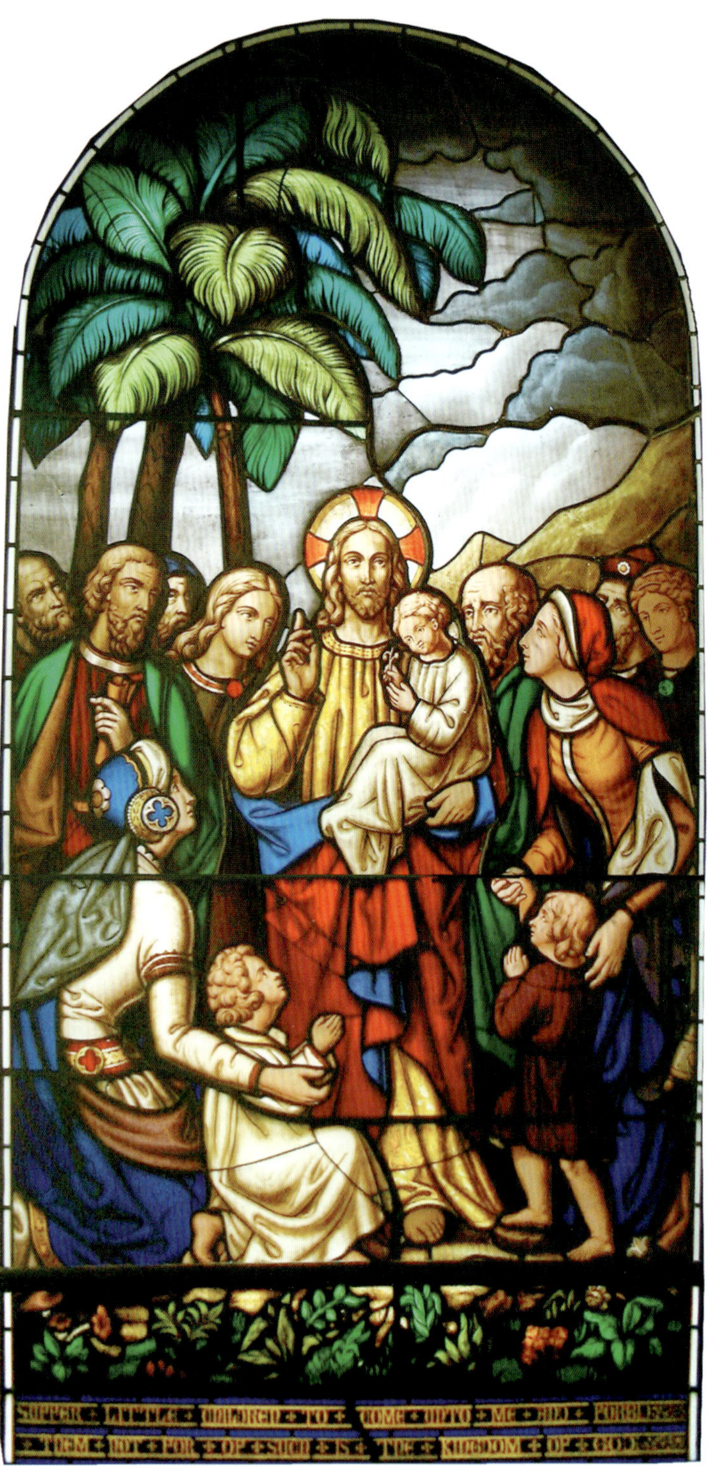

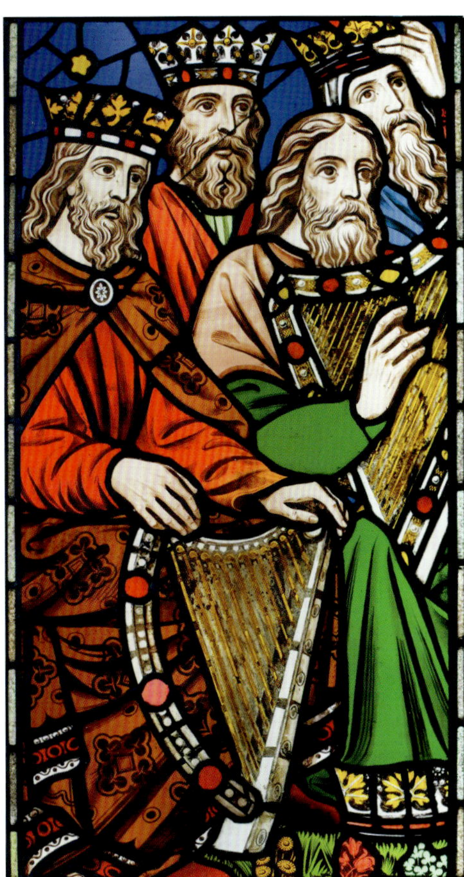

THE DANCE OF SALOME 1856
Designed and made by Antoine Lusson *fils* (son) (1840–76)

This lively panel is from a large four-light window depicting St John the Baptist's life and martyrdom: Salome was the young woman who persuaded King Herod to execute him.

Antoine Lusson *père* (father) was an important figure in the French Gothic Revival. In 1847 his Le Mans workshop was involved in the restoration of the 13th-century glass of the Sainte-Chapelle in Paris, the most important and prestigious project of its day. This window, one of the few works made by the Lusson studio in England, was removed from Ely Cathedral in the 1930s.

From the south (then north) choir aisle of Ely Cathedral. On loan from the Dean and Chapter of Ely Cathedral, 1986. (L1986.5.1)

THE ELDERS OF THE APOCALYPSE *c.*1857
Designed by William Butterfield (1814–1900); made by O'Connor & Sons

The church of All Saints, Margaret Street, was the great masterpiece of the Victorian Gothic Revival architect William Butterfield. He closely supervised every aspect of the decoration of his buildings and imposed his own distinctive style on the artists with whom he worked. The Agnus Dei window from which this panel comes was blocked up in about 1910, when an organ was installed in front of it. The window was removed in 1996 and as much as much glass as possible was relocated to the baptistery.

From the church of All Saints, Margaret Street, London W1. On loan from the Diocese of London, 1998. (L1998.3.2)

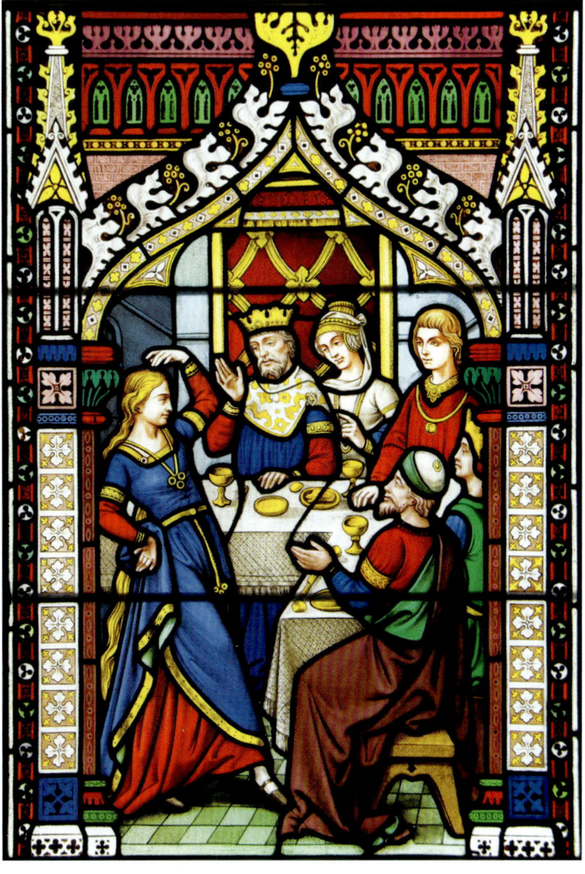

HIGH VICTORIAN REVIVAL

The full extent of the influence of the Gothic Revival on the stained glass industry was evident at the Great Exhibition of 1851 held in the Crystal Palace in London's Hyde Park. Twenty-five British studios exhibited in a gallery devoted to stained glass. With the exception of windows made by Hardman & Co. to Pugin's designs, which were shown in a separate Medieval Court, the British stained glass was generally considered inferior to the European exhibits. Windows in a wide variety of historic styles were displayed alongside pictorial enamel glass paintings. Barely a decade later pictorialism had almost disappeared and windows inspired by the two-dimensional Gothic art of the 13th and early 14th centuries dominated stained glass from the 1860s.

Following the example of Pugin and others, this medieval revival was taken up in the 1850s by a younger generation of architects and artists influenced by the Pre-Raphaelite movement. London stained glass studios Clayton & Bell, Heaton & Butler (later to become Heaton, Butler & Bayne) and Lavers & Barraud (later Lavers, Barraud & Westlake) were established in 1855 and employed in-house and freelance artist-designers. By the 1860s British stained glass had become pre-eminent in both design and quality of manufacture, and was exported all over the world. The high demand for stained glass and the pressure to keep up with production meant that window designs were frequently adapted and re-used.

ABOVE
REAP IN JOY 1870s
Designed by Nathaniel Hubert John Westlake (1833–1921); made by Lavers, Barraud & Westlake

This roundel is one of a pair based on a Psalm: 'Those who sow with tears will reap with songs of joy'. They were originally part of an east window positioned above a Crucifixion scene flanked by miracles in a chapel at the old hospital at Gloucester (now demolished).

Nathaniel Wood Lavers established a stained glass firm in 1855, the same year in which the firms Clayton & Bell and Heaton & Butler were formed. In 1858 he was joined by Francis Philip Barraud and in 1868 N.H.J. Westlake also became a partner. The firm continued to operate until 1921.

From the chapel of the Royal Hospital, Southgate Street, Gloucester. Donated by Gloucestershire Hospitals NHS Trust, 2015. (1985.4.1)

OPPOSITE, DETAIL
MOSES RETURNS FROM MOUNT SINAI 1863
Designed by John Milner Allen (active 1860s–80s); made by Lavers & Barraud

While early Methodist chapels were simple, often classical buildings, by the second half of the 19th century they were just as likely to be designed in the Gothic style and to be decorated with stained glass windows. J.M. Allen provided a large number of designs for Lavers & Barraud between 1861 and 1867. His work here is in a Gothic Revival style, but later he also produced designs in the Aesthetic style of the 1870s.

From Trinity Methodist Church, Wolverhampton, Staffordshire. Donated by the Minister and Congregation, 1976. (1976.2.1)

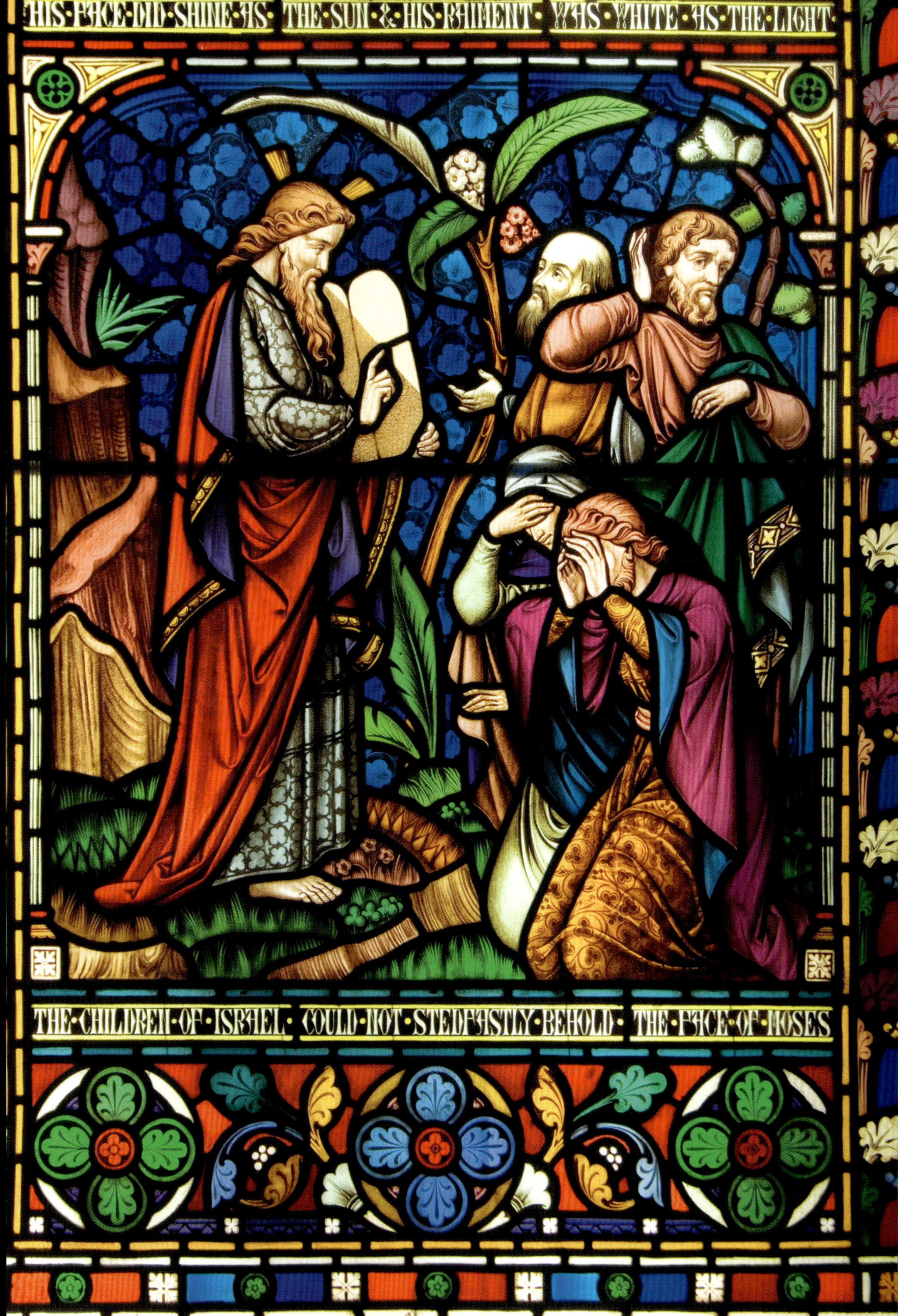

HIS FACE DID SHINE AS THE SUN & HIS RAIMENT WAS WHITE AS THE LIGHT
THE CHILDREN OF ISRAEL COULD NOT STEDFASTLY BEHOLD THE FACE OF MOSES

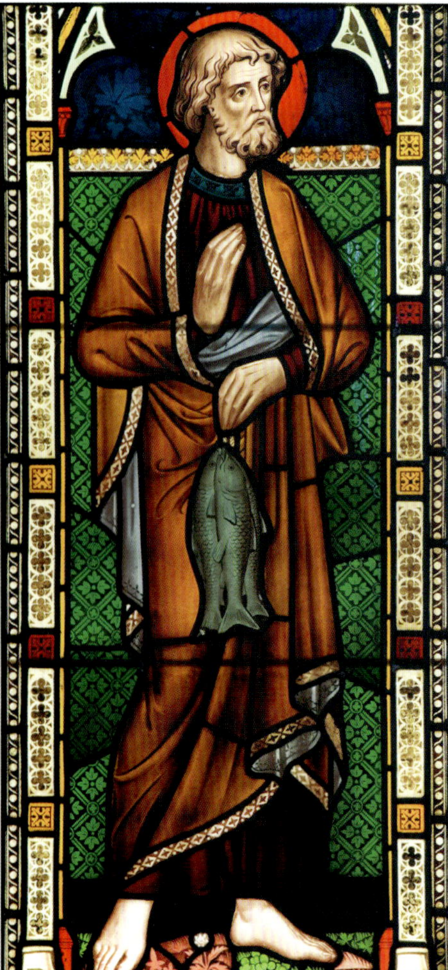

ST PETER THE EVANGELIST 1860s
Designed by Henry Stacy Marks (1829–98);
made by Lavers & Barraud

Henry Stacy Marks was a well-known painter
and decorative artist who designed stained glass
for both Clayton & Bell and Lavers & Barraud.
Here St Peter holds the fish that represents his
occupation as a fisherman and Christ's instruction
to him to become a 'fisher of men'.

Some of the purple glass has deteriorated to
such an extent that it has lost its translucency.
This condition, commonly called 'crizzling', is the
result of an imbalance of chemicals in the glass.

*From the church of St Michael, Queen Street, Derby.
Donated by the Derby Diocesan Advisory Committee,
1983.* (1983.19.1b)

THE GOOD SHEPHERD 1867
Designed and made by Charles Edmund Clutterbuck
(1806–61)

In this window the painterly figure in the landscape is
combined with the medieval framework of 13th-century
style foliage. C.E. Clutterbuck began his career as a
painter of miniatures in Stratford, East London. His
stained glass was almost exclusively pictorial in style.
Relatively little of his work survives in good condition,
partly because his glass was often inadequately fired.

*From Christ Church, Cotmanhay, Derbyshire.
Donated by the Diocese of Derby, 1987.* (1987.2.1)

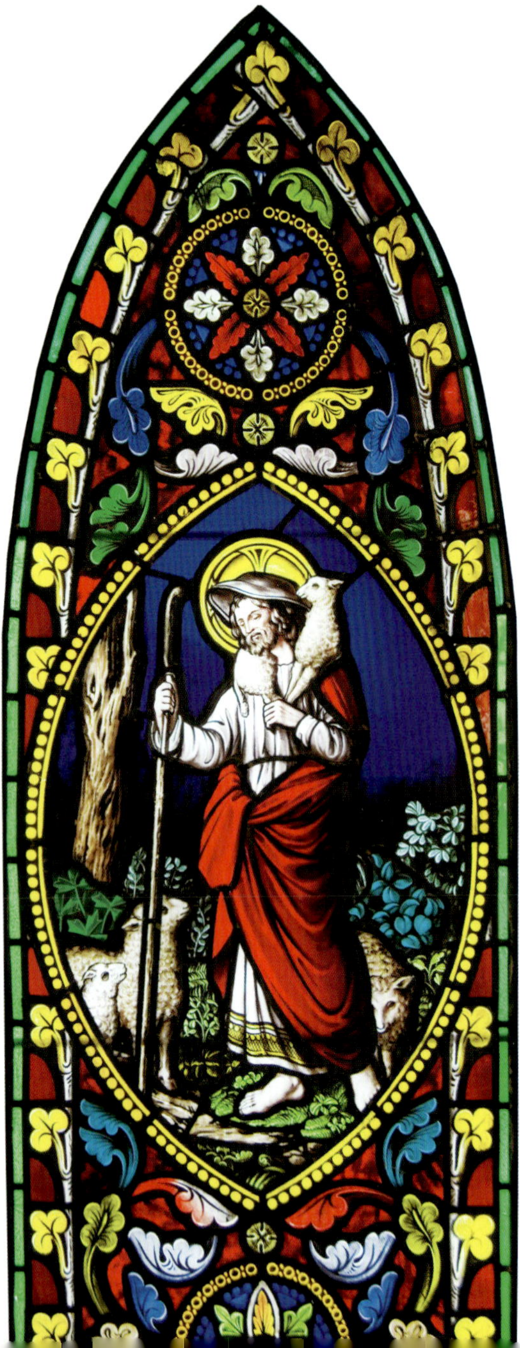

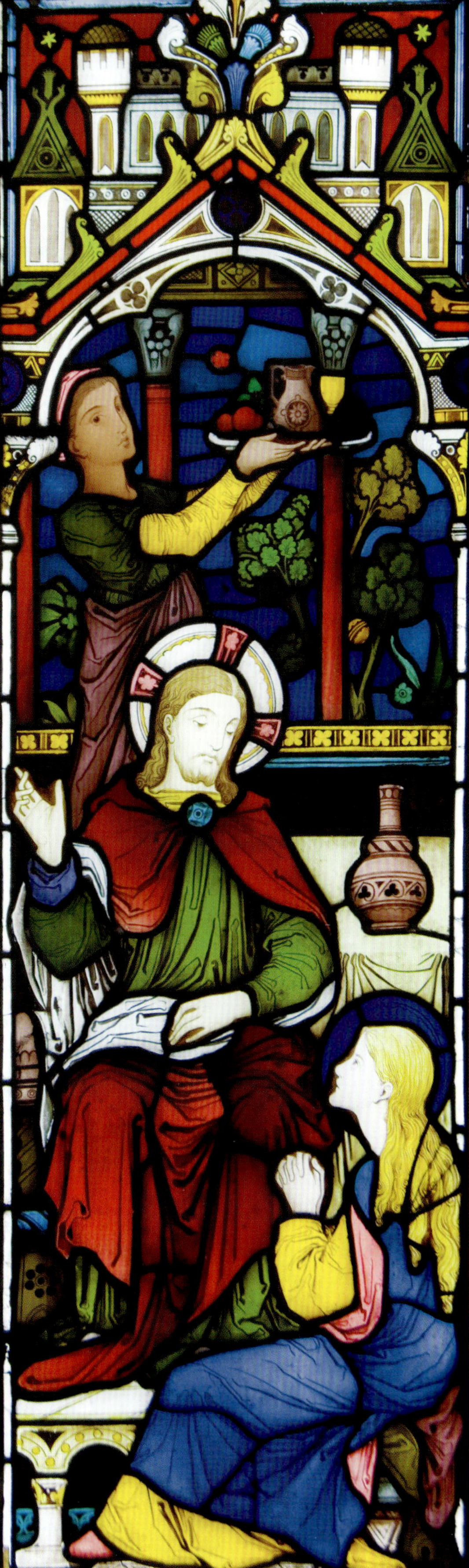

CHRIST IN THE HOUSE OF MARY AND MARTHA 1865
Designed by Robert Turnill Bayne (1837–1915); made by Heaton, Butler & Bayne

This window shows Martha, the busy housewife, and her sister Mary of Bethany, the quiet, thoughtful figure at the feet of Jesus. The window displays a strong, vigorous figure style and clear, bright colours associated with Heaton, Butler & Bayne. The ruby glass used in Christ's robe is particularly fine.

Clement Heaton and James Butler became partners in 1855 and were joined by Bayne in 1862. Heaton, Butler & Bayne became one of the largest and most successful stained glass firms in London.

From the church of St Andrew, Bridport, Dorset. Donated by the Diocese of Salisbury, 1979. (1979.2.2)

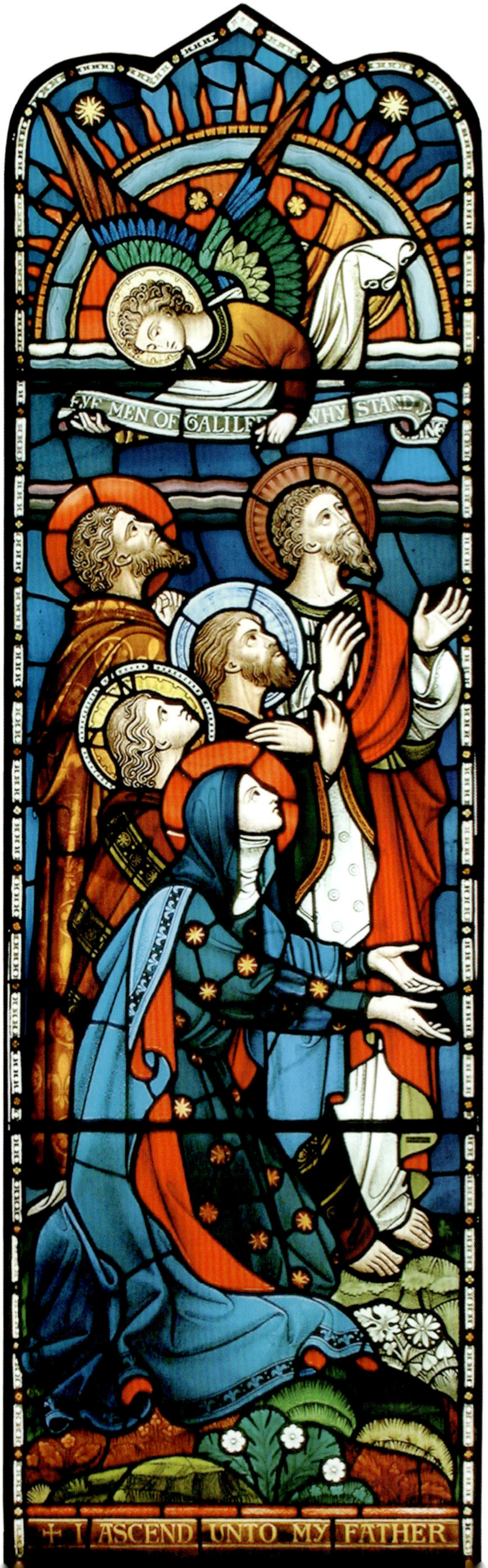

THE VIRGIN MARY AND DISCIPLES AT CHRIST'S ASCENSION 1861
Designed by John Richard Clayton (1827–1913); made by Clayton & Bell

This panel depicts Christ's Ascension into Heaven, witnessed by the Virgin Mary and the Disciples.

John Richard Clayton trained as an architectural draughtsman and began designing stained glass in 1853. He was also a sculptor and illustrator. In 1855 he and Alfred Bell founded the firm of Clayton & Bell, which become one of the most successful and prolific stained glass manufacturers of the Victorian period. This panel, with its bright colours, fluent draughtsmanship and bold leadwork, is typical of the firm's best early work.

From the church of St Peter the Great, Worcester. Donated by the Diocese of Worcester, 1976. (1976.3.1)

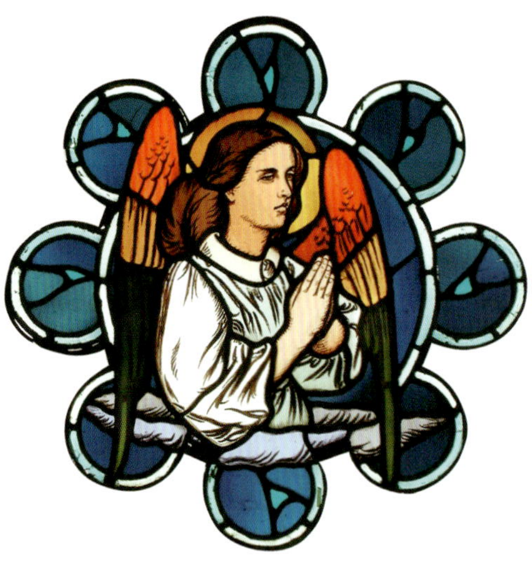

ANGEL 1863
Designed by John Hungerford Pollen (1820–1902); made by James Powell & Sons

The Church of the Assumption in Rhyl was built in 1863 for the growing local Roman Catholic population. J.H. Pollen designed the church, internal decoration and fittings. This panel was part of a rose window at the west end, which was demolished in 1976.

Pollen first worked with the members of the Pre-Raphaelite brotherhood in 1857, when he participated in the creation of the murals in the Oxford Union Debating Chamber. Like many Pre-Raphaelite designs, the angel seems to be based on a portrait, perhaps of a girl chorister.

From the church of the Assumption, Rhyl, Denbighshire. Purchased 1976. (1976.8.2)

REYNARD THE FOX 1870s

Designed and made by Clement
James Heaton (1824–82)

This panel, made for Eaton Hall
during a rebuilding of the manor
house by architect Alfred Waterhouse,
demonstrates the popularity of
stained glass in Victorian domestic
contexts. Set in monogrammed
quarries, the central roundel depicts
a scene from Aesop's Fables also
popular in the Middle Ages. The 'W'
surmounted by a ducal crown refers
to the 1st Duke of Westminster,
Hugh Lupus Grosvenor, whose
heraldry includes the wheatsheaf.
The wolf in the border is a rebus
(picture of a word) for his middle
name, meaning 'wolf' in Latin.

*From the entrance hall of Eaton Hall,
Cheshire. Purchased 1996.* (1996.3)

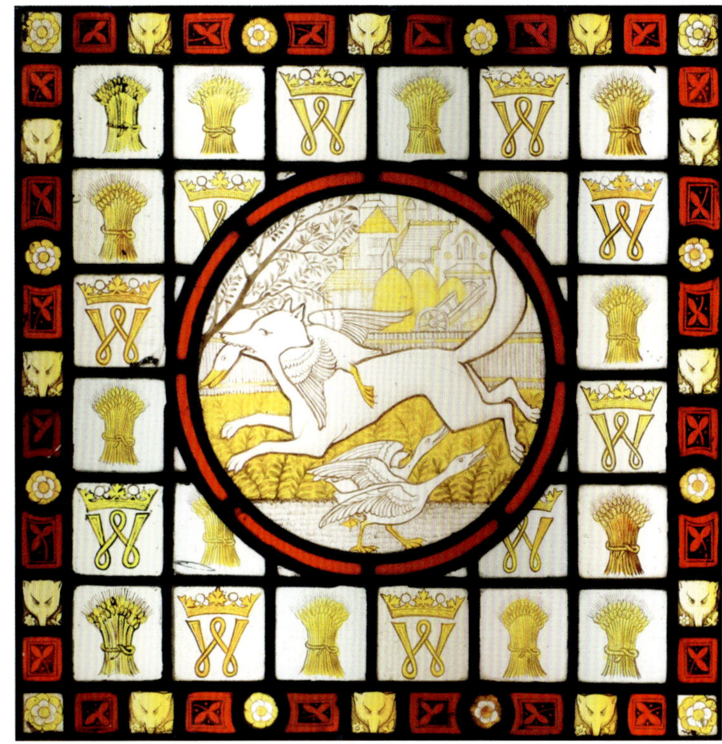

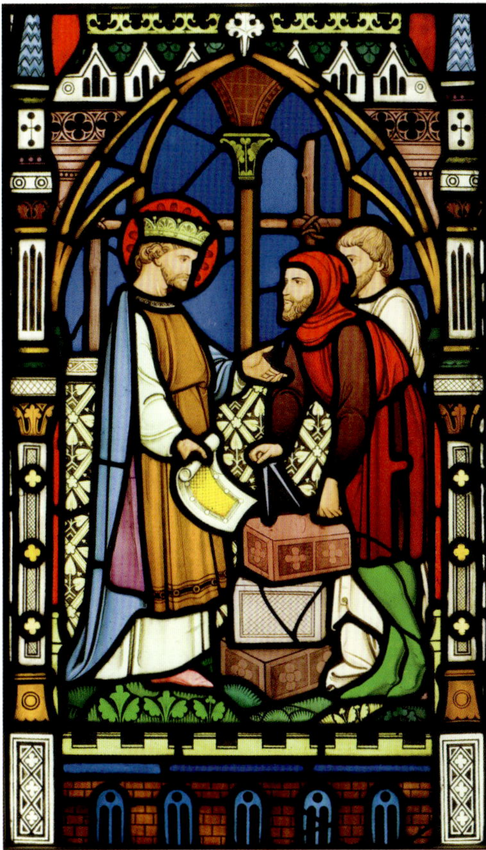

SOLOMON SUPERVISES THE BUILDING OF THE TEMPLE *c.*1860

Design attributed to John Richard
Clayton (1827–1913); made by
Clayton & Bell

Solomon was renowned for his great
wisdom. The temple at Jerusalem
was constructed during his reign and
he is often depicted overseeing the
work. This panel, with its rich colour
and 14th-century style canopies
and borders, combines the strong
design and expert craftsmanship
typical of Clayton & Bell's work after
1859. Some of the glass may well be
Powell's antique, which was made
using recipes derived from Charles
Winston's experiments of the late
1840s on the nature and composition
of medieval glass.

*From the church of Holy Trinity,
Beaminster, Dorset. Donated by Whiteway
& Waldron Ltd, 1980.* (1980.11)

SCOTTISH STAINED GLASS

The Reformation in Scotland came later than in England but its impact was far more destructive. Religious strife, neglect and a gradual loss of skill in the craft over a period of 250 years resulted in the virtual elimination of medieval stained glass from Scotland. The Gothic Revival in Scotland began relatively late in the 19th century and from the outset Scottish artists were far more responsive to Continental Art Nouveau than their English counterparts. By the 1890s Glasgow had emerged as Scotland's artistic centre. Both Daniel Cottier and Charles Rennie Mackintosh gained international reputations. The firm of J. & W. Guthrie employed a succession of talented freelance designers who produced exciting and distinctive stained glass. Two of the most highly regarded Scottish designers, David Gauld and J. Harrington-Mann, are represented in the Museum's collection.

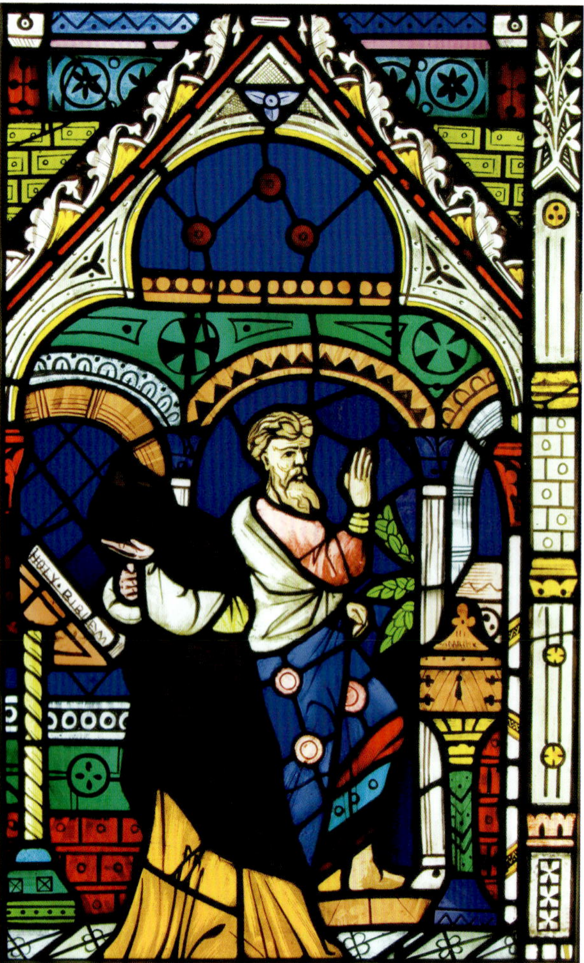

LEFT
THE PARABLE OF THE PHARISEE AND THE PUBLICAN 1865
Designed by Daniel Cottier (1838–91); made by Field & Allan

The architectural framework of this angular and expressive panel is based on the 14th-century style but the bright colours are much bolder than a medieval palette. It is probably an early design by Daniel Cottier, who trained in Glasgow, Edinburgh and London, where he was influenced by John Ruskin and the Pre-Raphaelites. He managed Field & Allan, based in Edinburgh and Leith, before setting up an independent studio in Edinburgh in 1864, later relocating to London. Cottier & Co. was internationally successful, with branches in New York, Melbourne and Sydney in the 1870s.

From Trinity Church, Irvine, Ayrshire. Donated by the Irvine Development Corporation, 1976. (1976.9.5)

OPPOSITE, DETAIL
CHRIST AND HIS FOLLOWERS *c.*1885
Designed by Alexander Walker (active 1896–1929); made by Adam & Small

Adam & Small made some of Scotland's finest windows in the 1870s and 1880s, with a strongly neoclassicist Aesthetic style and a distinctive range of colours, as seen in this panel. Stephen Adam worked in Cottier & Co.'s Edinburgh studio until 1870, when he entered into a partnership with David Small. Adam had studied medieval and modern stained glass in Europe and was influenced by the works of Burne-Jones and Holman Hunt. He was also inspired by Japanese art, imported into Europe from the late 1860s.

From the church of St James, Leith. Donated by Pendrich (Steeplejacks) Ltd, 1980. (1980.16)

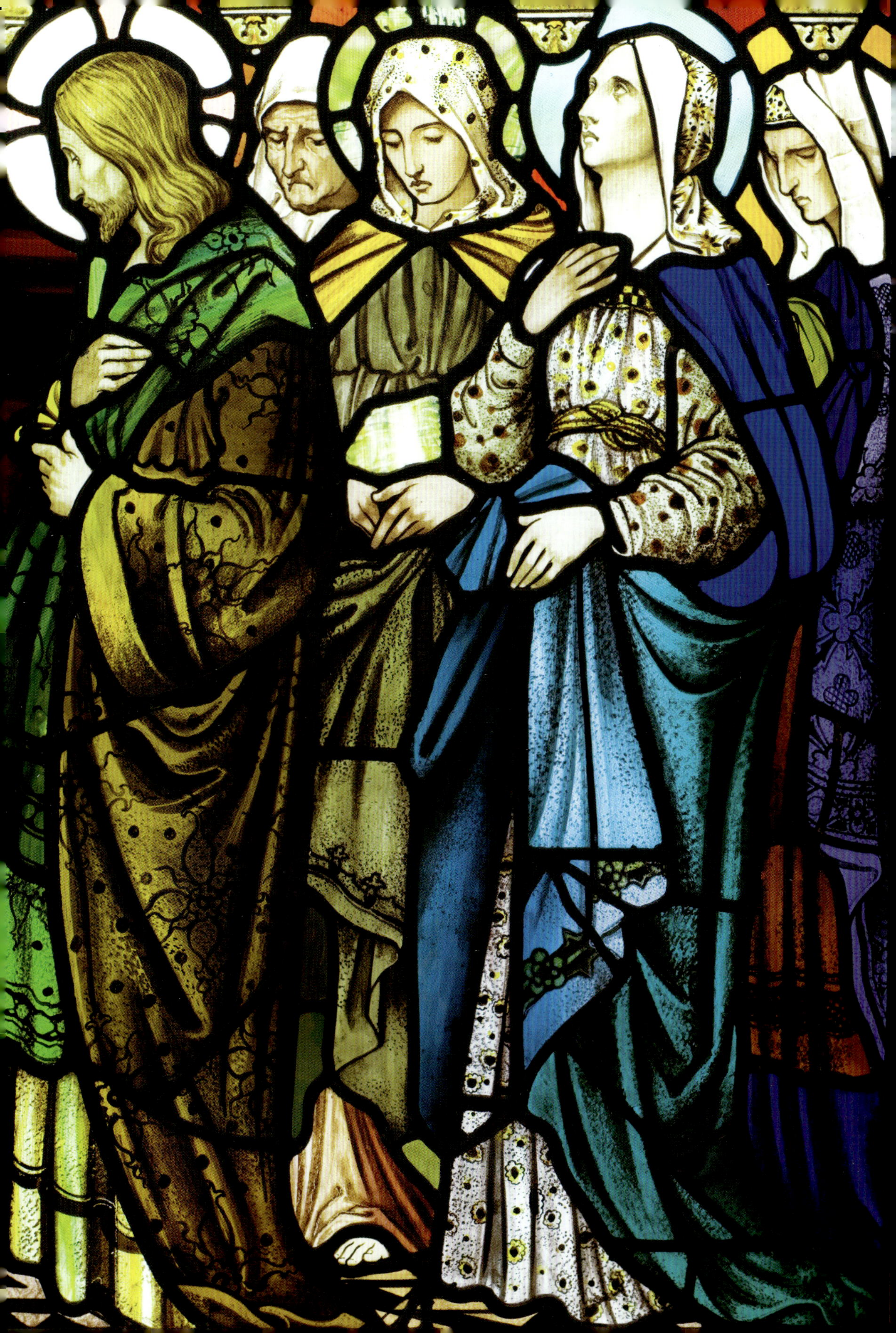

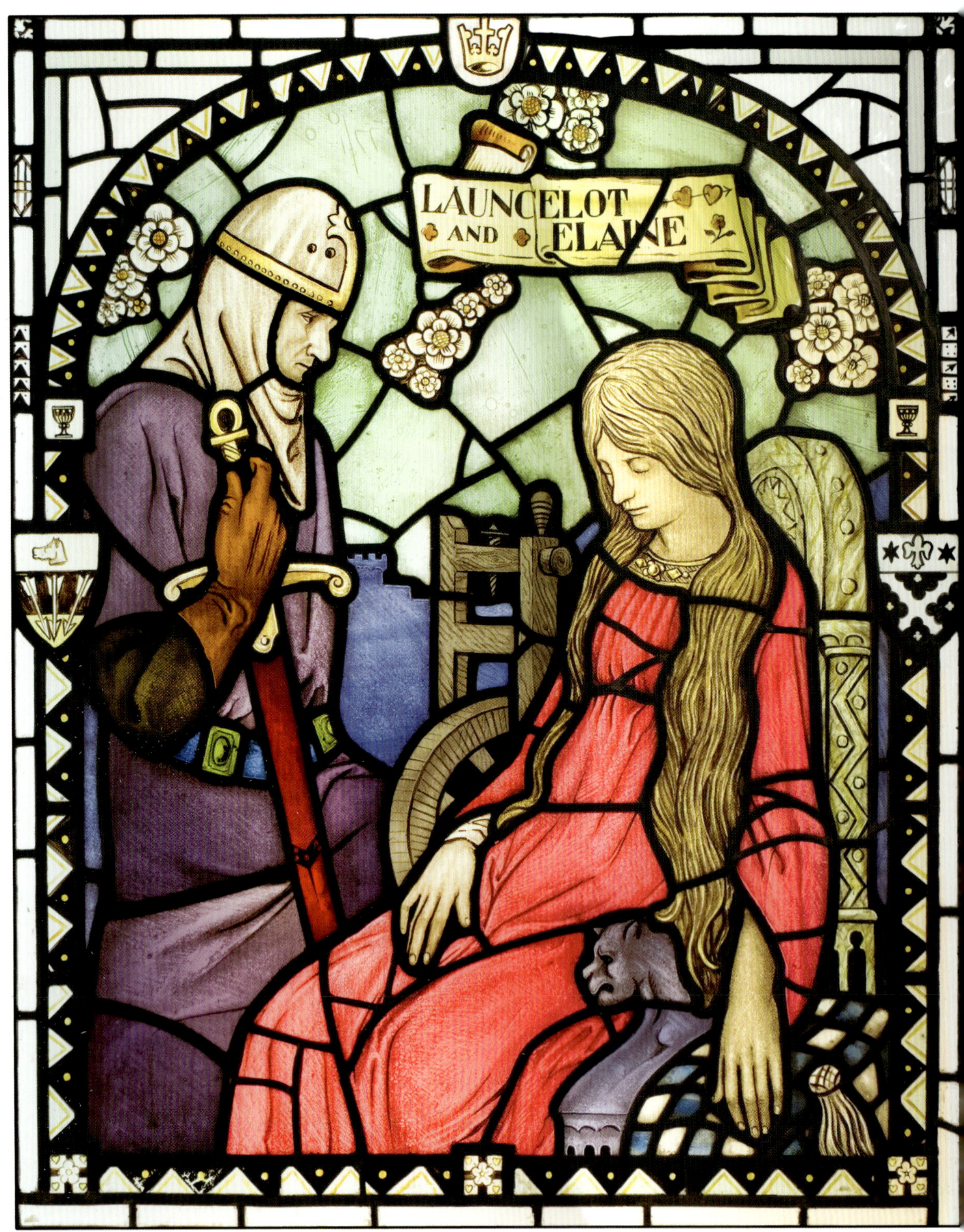

LAUNCELOT AND ELAINE

LAUNCELOT AND ELAINE *c.*1910
Designed and made by Andrew Stoddart
(1876–1940)

The chivalric tales of King Arthur were popular
in the 19th and early 20th centuries, especially
for secular settings. This panel, closely based on
a tapestry design by the German Art Nouveau
designer J.H. Vogeler (1872–1942), illustrates
Elaine, 'the Lily Maid of Astolat', discovering that
her love for Sir Lancelot is unrequited.

Born in Scotland, Stoddart was influenced
by the Glasgow school of designers and the Art
Nouveau movement. He established a studio
in Nottingham in the early 1900s and made this
panel for his own home.

From the artist's home, Nottingham.
Donated by the Page family, 1977. (1977.1)

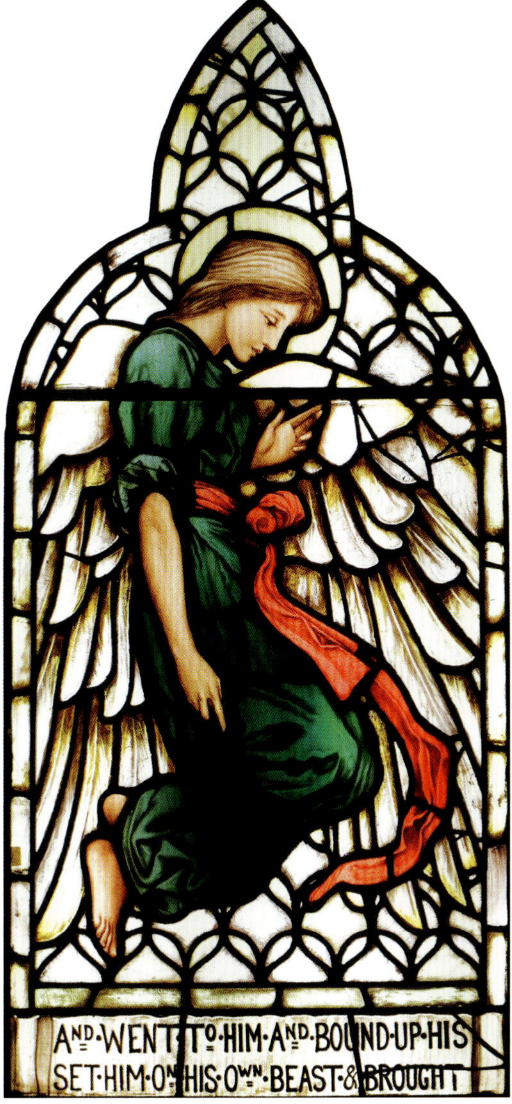

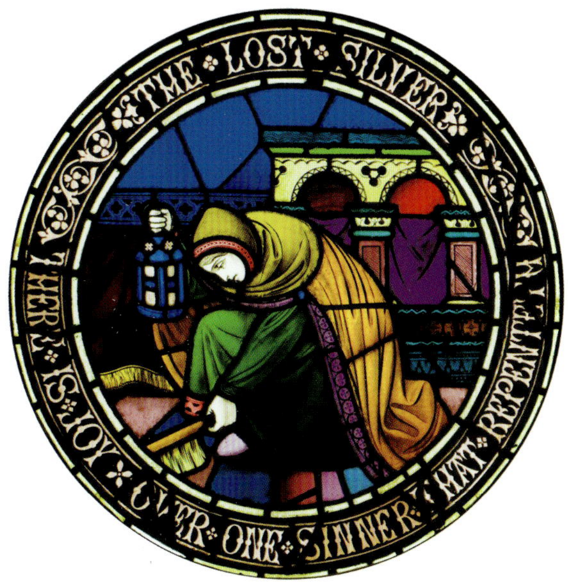

THE PARABLE OF THE LOST COIN 1865
Designed and made by James Tennant Lyon
(1836–72)

James Tennant Lyon worked as a freelance
designer for James Powell & Sons from 1857,
before setting up his own studio in 1864. He
later collaborated with the designer William de
Morgan, executing his stained glass designs.
This panel, depicting one of the Parables told
by Jesus in his teaching ministry, came from
a redundant church in Glasgow. The full-scale
cartoon for this panel is also in the Museum's
collection.

From Trinity Church, Irvine, Ayrshire. Donated by
the Irvine Development Corporation, 1976. (1976.9.1)

KNEELING ANGEL 1893
Designed by Harrington Mann (1864–1937);
made by J. & W. Guthrie

The firm of J. & W. Guthrie was established in 1850 by
decorative painter John Guthrie senior, a founder member
of the Art Workers Guild, and continued by his sons John
and William. The firm began making stained glass in
1884, employing a number of talented young designers.
Harrington Mann, a member of The Glasgow Boys noted
for his landscape and portrait paintings, began designing
for the Guthries in the 1890s. These panels demonstrate
the Art Nouveau elegance and sensitive approach to
colour of his outstanding stained glass designs.

After its conversion into a concert hall for the Scottish
National Orchestra, several windows from Trinity Church,
Claremont Street, Glasgow, were given to the Museum.
Sadly, some windows were accidentally destroyed during
building works.

From Trinity Church, Claremont Street, Glasgow. Donated by
the Scottish National Orchestra, 1978. (1978.3.1)

NEW INSPIRATION: WILLIAM MORRIS AND HIS CIRCLE

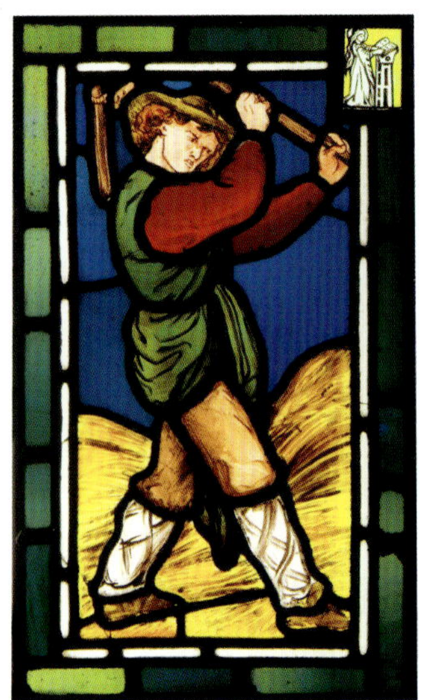

In 1861 close friends and collaborators William Morris and Edward Burne-Jones established the firm of Morris, Marshall, Faulkner & Co. in partnership with artists Dante Gabriel Rossetti and Ford Madox Brown, the architect Philip Webb and others. Their aim was to rescue the decorative arts from commercialisation and industrial methods of production. A subtle and original use of colour and a fresh approach to design characterised their work, which encompassed furniture, tiles, wallpaper, textiles and stained glass. Burne-Jones's skills as a draughtsman and interest in Italian renaissance art was combined with Morris's talent for pattern, seen in his wallpapers and textiles and in his colourful, rich foliage in the firm's stained glass. The original partnership was dissolved in 1875 and the reorganised firm renamed Morris & Co.

Following the example of Burne-Jones, the work of artists such as Henry Holiday exemplified these new influences. Holiday introduced the sculptural, classical styles of Greece and Rome and of the Italian Renaissance to stained glass produced by James Powell & Sons, where he succeeded Burne-Jones as chief designer, and Lavers & Barraud. Other influential artists began to transform the art through the introduction of a new stylistic vocabulary influenced by Japanese art and design.

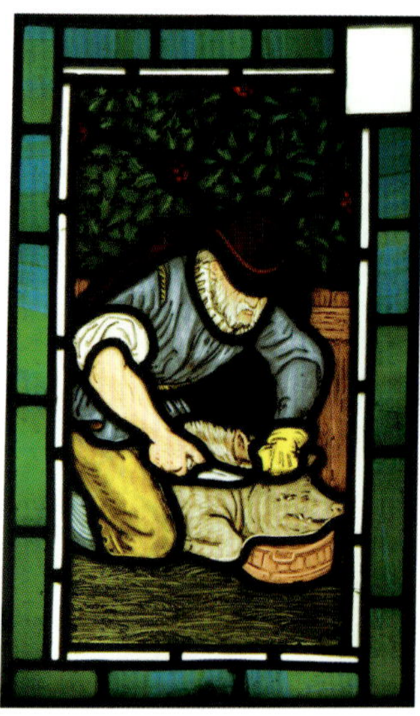

LABOURS OF THE MONTHS: AUGUST, THRESHING AND DECEMBER, KILLING A HOG 1863

Designed by Dante Gabriel Rossetti (1828–82); made by Morris, Marshall, Faulkner & Co.

These two panels, designed by Pre-Raphaelite painter Dante Gabriel Rossetti, were once part of a set of 12 Labours of the Months. They came from the drawing room of Silsden House, built for Bradford textile manufacturer Charles Hastings to the designs of architect Richard Norman Shaw. Although the glass was removed before Silsden was demolished in 1903, only these panels and 'March', now in the collection of the William Morris Gallery, survive.

From Silsden House, Keighley, Yorkshire. Donated by Nicholas Godlee, 2001. (2002.2.1 and 2002.2.2)

OPPOSITE, DETAIL

KING DAVID *c.*1865–72

Designed and made by William de Morgan (1839–1917)

William de Morgan was a distinguished designer, ceramicist and novelist who began designing tiles and stained glass for Morris & Co. in the 1860s. He shared premises with James Tennant Lyon in Fitzroy Square, London, from around 1865 until 1872, but after a kiln fire established an independent pottery studio in Chelsea, later relocating to Merton and then Fulham.

David, the shepherd boy who killed the giant Goliath, is here depicted in his equally familiar guise as the musician king of Israel. This window, one of several made for Little Stanmore church, was removed in the 1970s during a restoration that returned the church to its Georgian appearance.

From the church of St Lawrence, Little Stanmore, Middlesex. Donated by the Parochial Church Council, 1978. (1978.9.1)

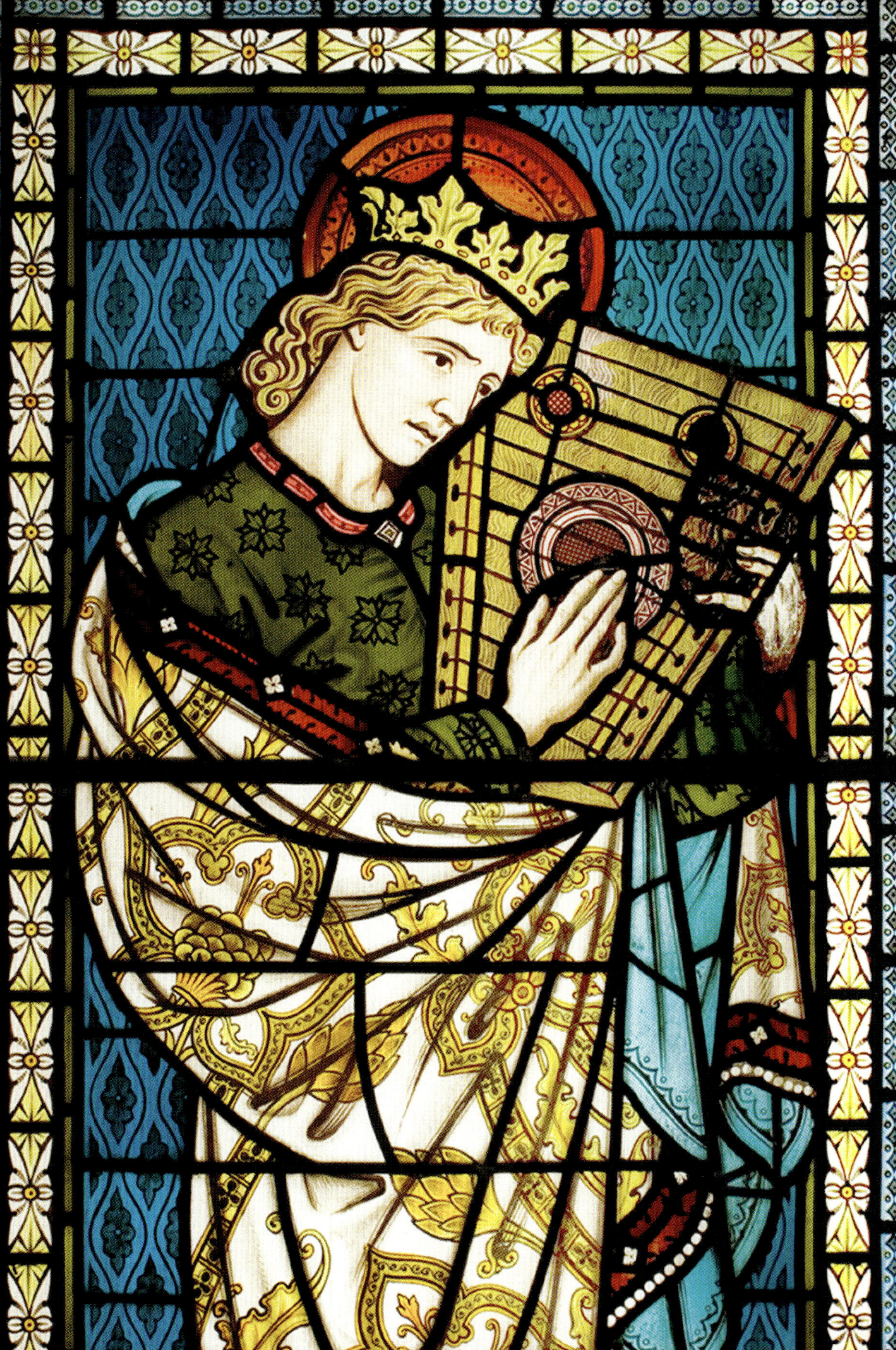

MUSICIAN ANGEL 1865

Designed by Edward Burne-Jones (1833–98);
made by Morris, Marshall, Faulkner & Co.

One of Burne-Jones's early designs for Morris, Marshall,
Faulkner & Co., this reveals his strong ability in this
medium. The original cartoon is in Birmingham Museum
and Art Gallery. The panel was once one of the uppermost
tracery lights of a large window in the east wall of Christ
Church, Bishopwearmouth, in the Diocese of Durham.
The same design was used for a window at the church
of St John the Baptist, Morton, Lincolnshire.

*From Christ Church, Bishopwearmouth, County Durham.
Donated by the Diocese of Durham, 2007.* (2007.2)

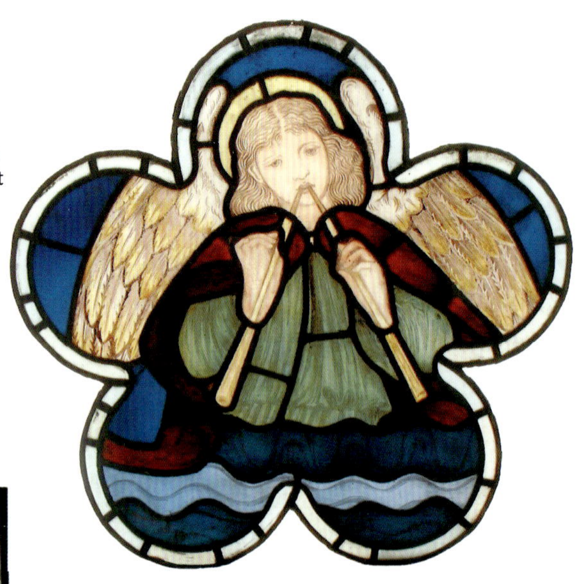

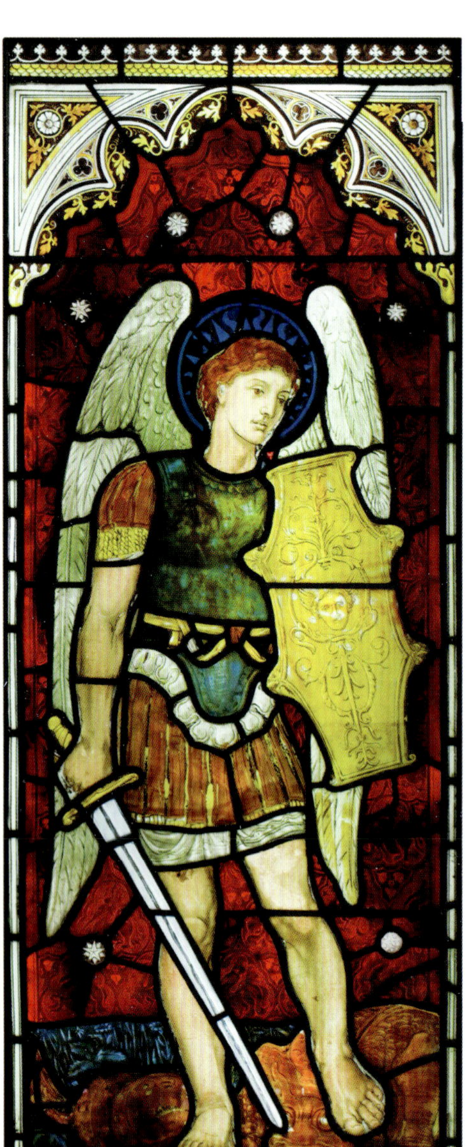

ST MICHAEL 1876

Designed by Harry Ellis Wooldridge
(1845–1917); made by James Powell
& Sons

St Michael is one of the four archangels
named in the Bible. Frequently depicted
fighting the forces of evil, his wings
distinguish him from St George, the
patron saint of England. In the 1860s
Wooldridge worked as studio assistant
to Edward Burne-Jones and later with
Henry Holiday. He succeeded John
Ruskin as Slade Professor of Art at
Oxford and was also a significant figure
in the study of medieval and renaissance
music. Wooldridge's neoclassical figure
style is combined here with delicate
modelling and subtle colours. Poor firing
of the glass may have resulted in the
deterioration of the paint, some of which
has been lost over time.

*From the church of St Michael and All Angels,
Weybridge, Surrey. Donated by the Guildford
Diocesan Advisory Committee, 1973.* (1973.2.1)

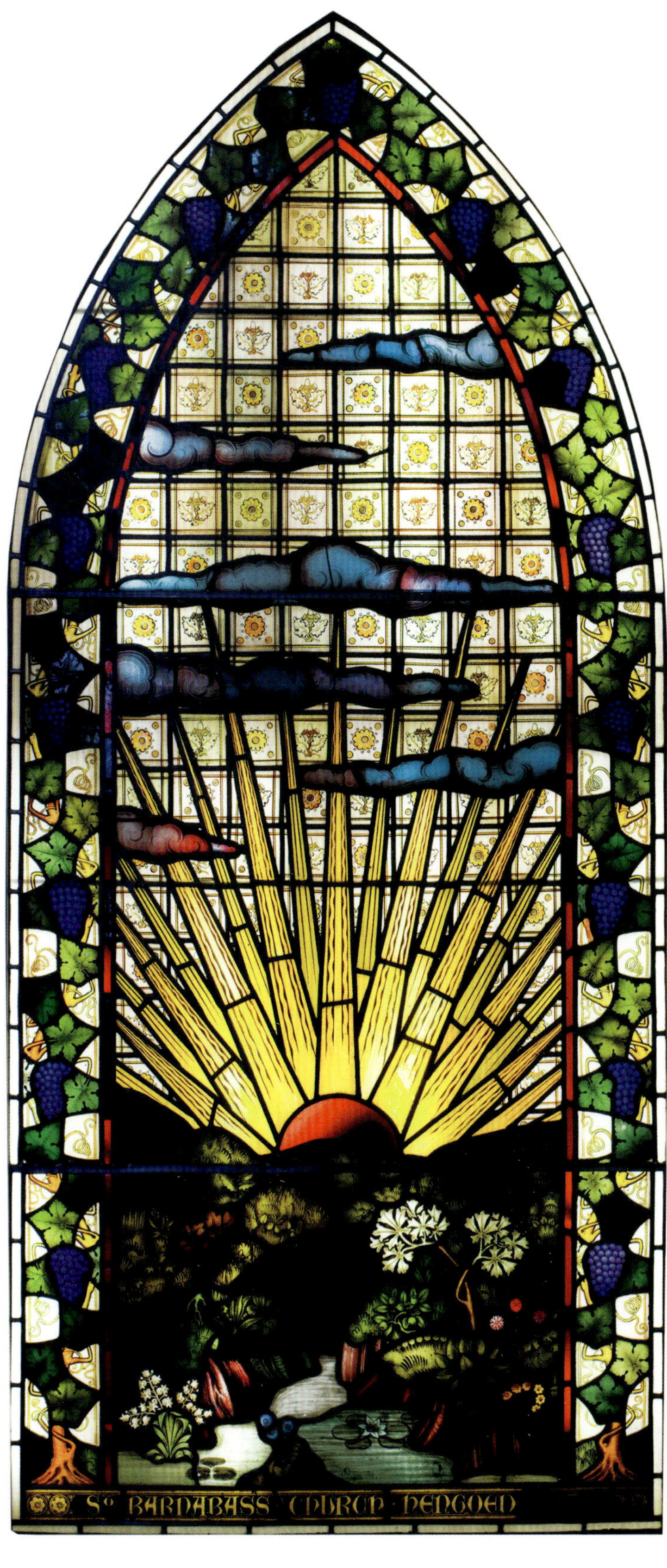

THE DAWNING OF THE LAST DAY
1871

Designed and made by Frederick Ashwin (1835–1909)

This window, Ashwin's only recorded work in Britain, is a memorial to Charles Arthur Albany Lloyd, Rector of Whittington, a parish on the Welsh border. It is a fine example of the Aesthetic idiom in stained glass, which rejected the forms of the Gothic Revival in favour of more original motifs, sometimes drawn from Japanese or ancient Greek art. Shortly after making this window Ashwin left for Sydney, where he set up one of Australia's first stained glass studios, Ashwin & Falconer.

From the church of St Barnabas, Hengoed, Shropshire. On loan from Mr A. Kenyon. (L1999.3)

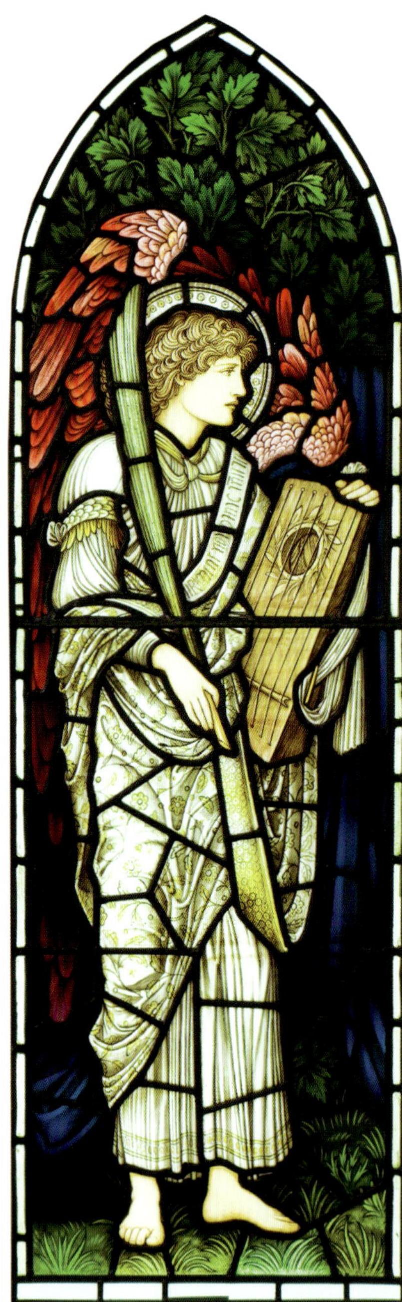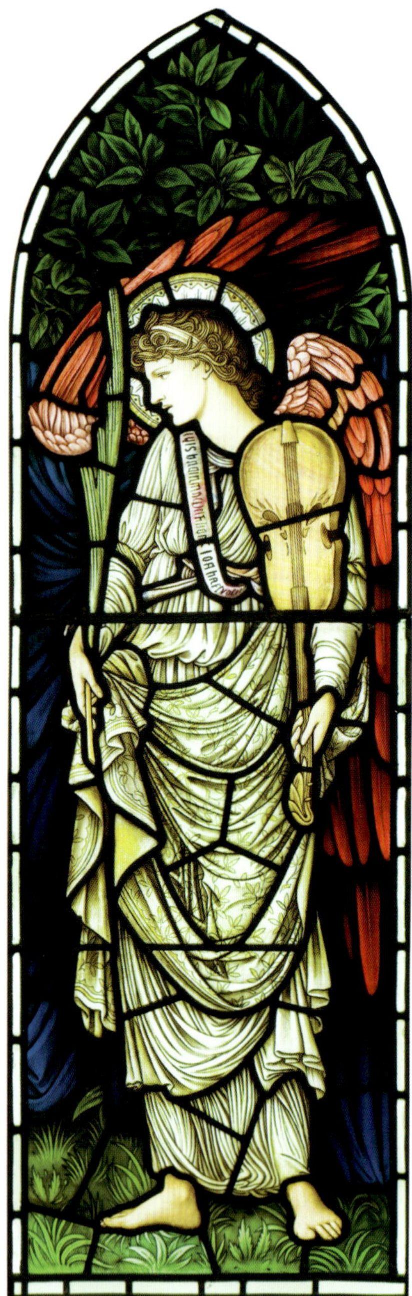

ANGEL MUSICIANS DESIGNED 1875, MADE 1910–12
Designed by Edward Burne-Jones (1833–98); made by Morris & Co.

First used for a window in Christ Church Cathedral, Oxford, in 1875, these angels are in Burne-Jones's Italianate style from the 1870s. The designs were later re-used many times by Morris & Co. During the 1880s Burne-Jones's style underwent a significant change. His later, monumental windows in Birmingham Cathedral show the profound impact of Byzantine mosaics, both in the hieratic, elongated figure drawing and in the use of small pieces of glass and dense, assertive patterns of lead.

From The Old Meeting, Bristol Street, Birmingham. On loan from the Dean and Chapter of Coventry Cathedral, 1975. (L1975.4.2+3)

SUFFER THE LITTLE CHILDREN DESIGNED 1892, MADE 1907
Designed and made by Henry Holiday (1839–1927)

The Unitarians had long suffered religious persecution, but during the 19th century they emerged as a Nonconformist denomination that attracted some of the wealthiest and best-educated patrons of the arts. This panel, from a large window depicting scenes from Christ's ministry, was given in memory of the Durning-Lawrence family, who were great Unitarian philanthropists.

Inspired by his travels in Italy in 1867, Holiday's style became increasingly classical. His involvement with the Arts and Crafts movement led him to experiment with making his own glass. He was particularly partial to slab glass, its uneven surface creating a jewel-like effect.

From Essex Unitarian Church, Notting Hill, London. Donated by Essex Unitarian Church, 1973. (1973.3.1)

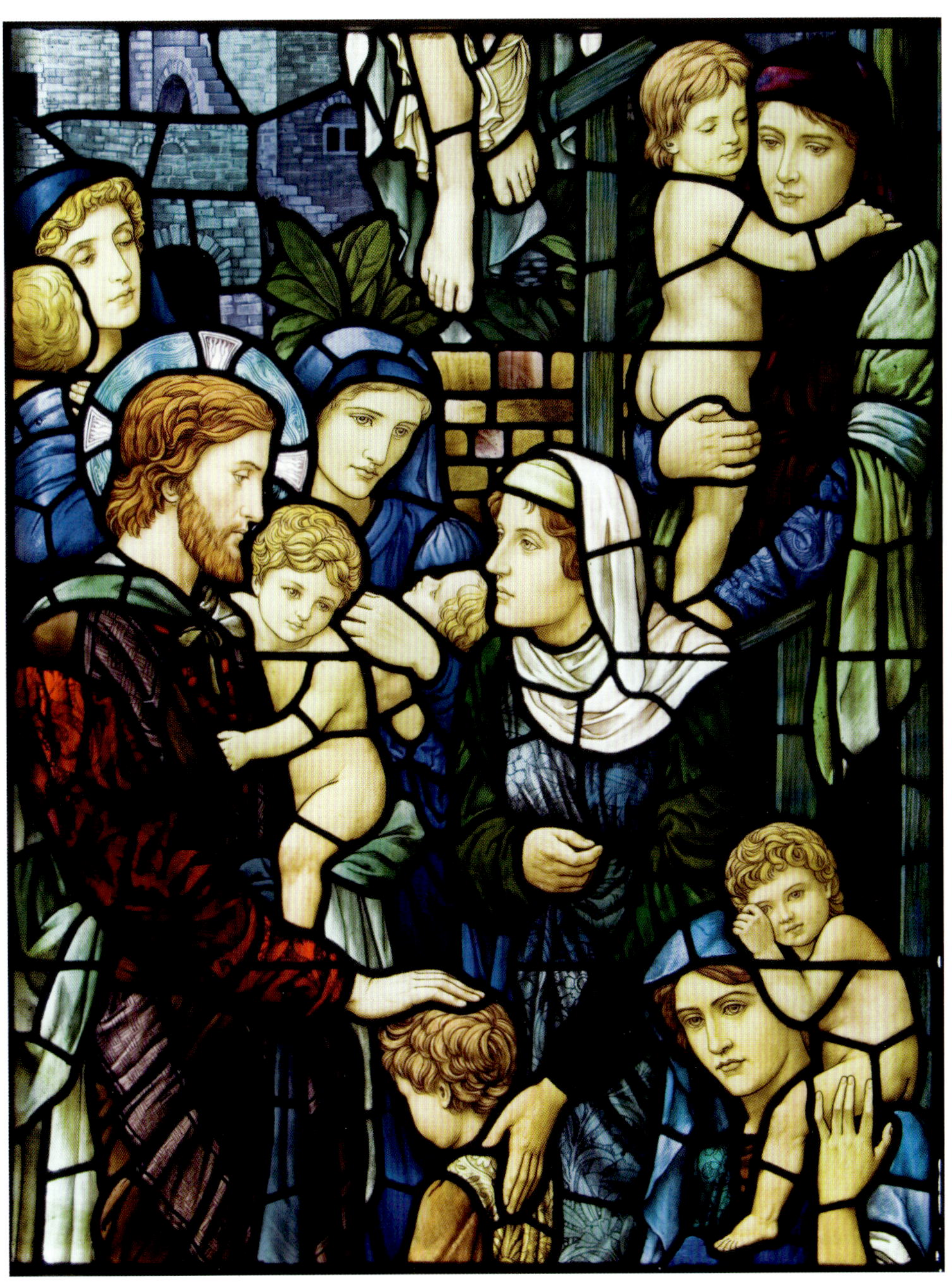

THE ARTS AND CRAFTS MOVEMENT

The 1880s saw the emergence of a younger generation of artists and craft workers who reacted against large-scale commercial studio practice and committed themselves to putting artistry and craftsmanship on an equal footing, often working independently in small-scale studios. Christopher Whall was an influential artist and teacher at the Central School of Arts and Crafts and the Royal College of Art and the work of many of his pupils can be seen in the Museum's collection. His inspirational *Stained Glass Work: A Text-book for Students and Workers in Glass* (1905) was used by generations of artists across the world.

Arts and Crafts artists had a deep interest in the material of glass and its effects. From its development in 1889, slab glass, developed by London glass firm of Britten & Gilson under the encouragement architect E.S. Prior, became the favourite raw material of Arts and Crafts stained glass artists. 'Prior's Early English' slab glass was blown into a box-shaped mould, producing a five-sided rectangular bottle. Cutting this along its edges produced five small sheets of uneven thickness, which gave its colour exceptional intensity and a sparkling, jewel-like quality.

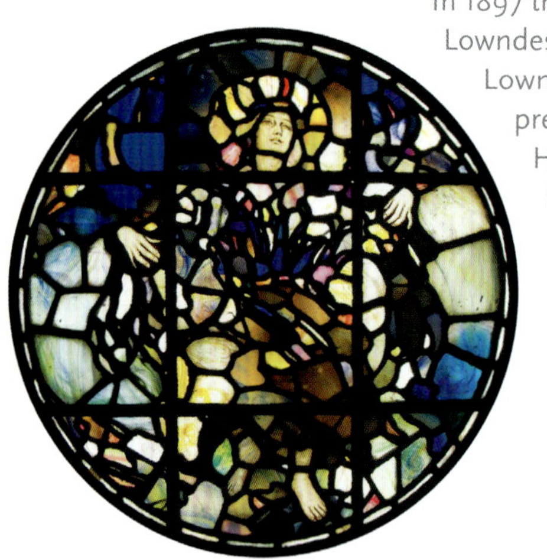

In 1897 the artist and campaigner for women's suffrage Mary Lowndes and craftsman Alfred Drury founded the firm of Lowndes & Drury; in 1906 they moved to custom-built premises in Lettice Street in Fulham, London. The Glass House, as it was known, became an important centre for British Arts and Crafts stained glass: designers could rent a studio and make use of the kiln facilities and expertise of the staff. It was especially valuable to the growing number of talented women artists drawn to stained glass.

COMMERCE 1923
Designed and made by Leonard Walker (1877–1964)

A replica of the centre of a window made for the Hong Kong and Shanghai Bank in Singapore. The complete window measured 5m wide by 2m high and was one of many made for the Bank on the theme of global trade. Before being shipped to Singapore, several stained glass panels from the scheme were exhibited in Selfridges London store in 1924. Walker relied heavily on the texture and colour of the 'streaky' slab glass, which was manufactured especially for him. He used paint only sparingly for the hands, feet and face of this allegorical figure.

Replica of a panel made for the Hong Kong and Shanghai Bank, Collyer Quay, Singapore. Donated by Renton M. Walker, 1981. (1981.6)

OPPOSITE
THE PARABLE OF THE RICH FOOL 1898
Designed by James Clark (1858–1943);
made by Arthur J. Dix

This parable illustrates the dangers of greed. Clark's travels in the Holy Land provided details for the costume and other decoration. The 'seedy', shimmering appearance of the glass was achieved by trapping air bubbles in the mixture. Clark was a versatile and successful artist; these were his first designs for stained glass. He studied at the Central School of Arts and Crafts to gain a better understanding of how stained glass windows were made and his designs were then skilfully translated into stained glass by Arthur J. Dix.

From the church of St John, Windermere. Donated by Carlisle Diocesan Redundant Churches Uses Committee, 1992. (1999.2)

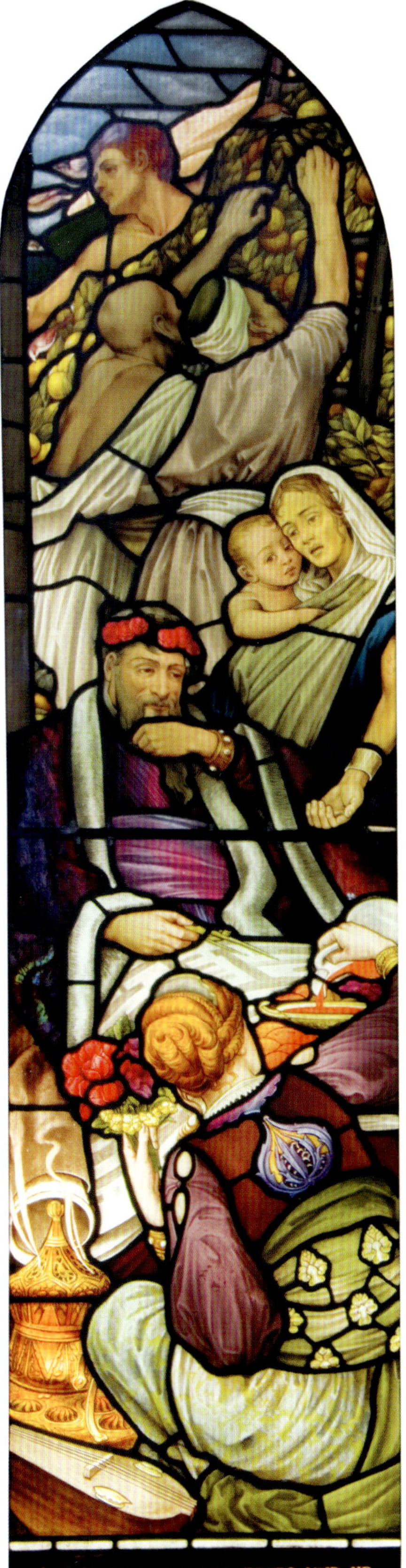
SOUL·THOU·HAST·MUCH·GOODS·LAID·UP
EAT·DRINK·AND·BE·MERRY

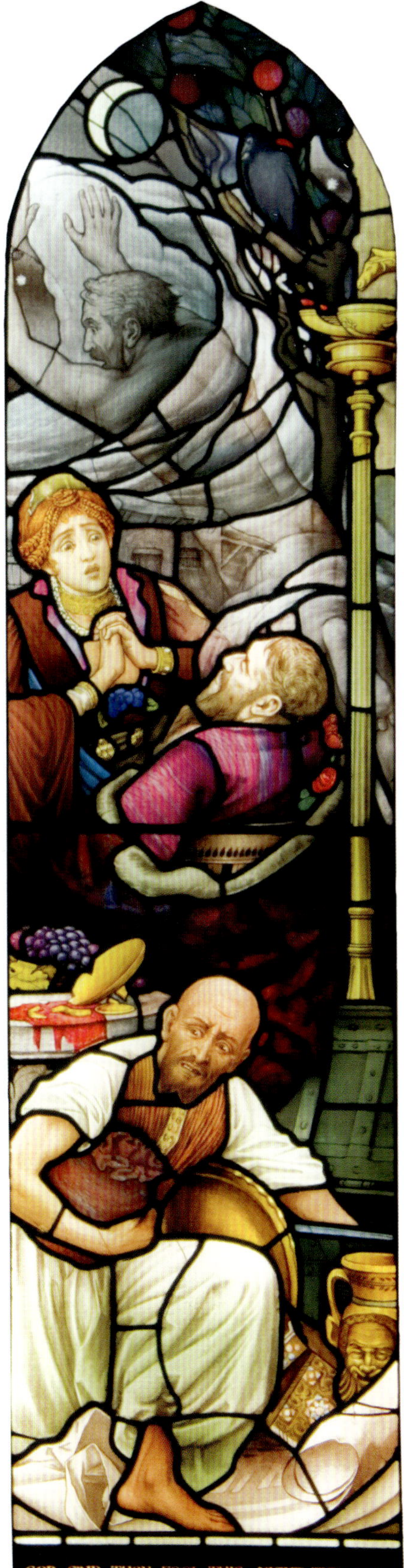
GOD·SAID·THOU·FOOL·THIS·NIGHT·THY·SOUL
SHALL·BE·REQUIRED·OF·THEE

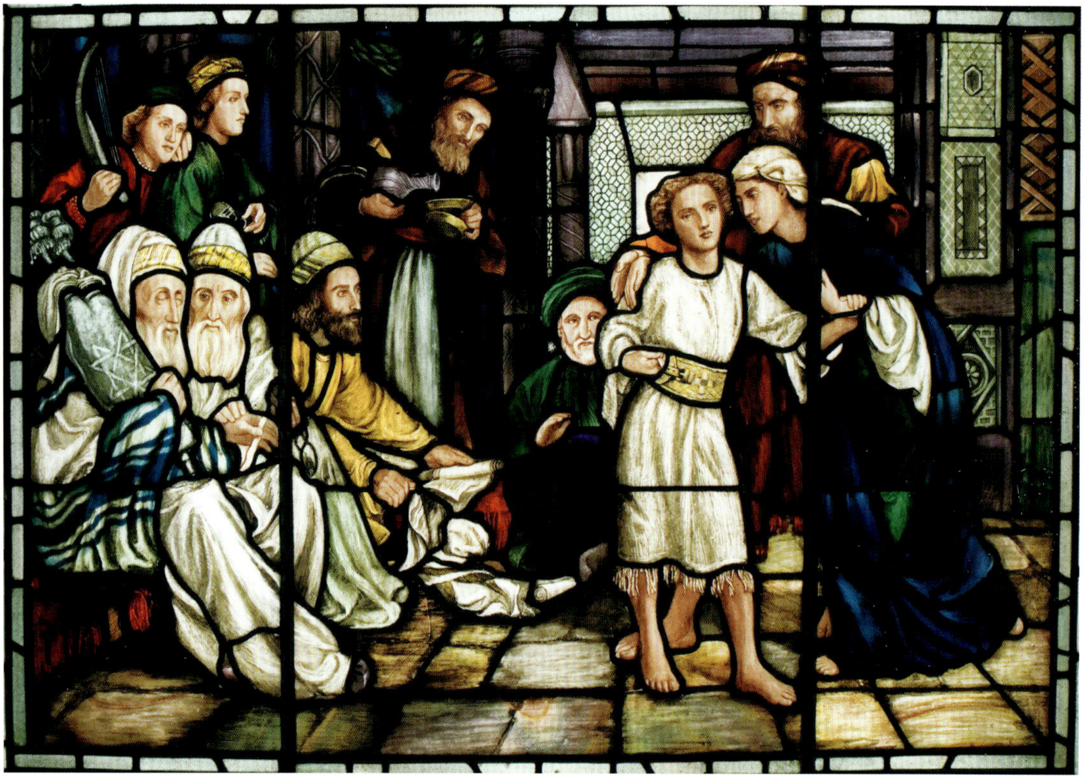

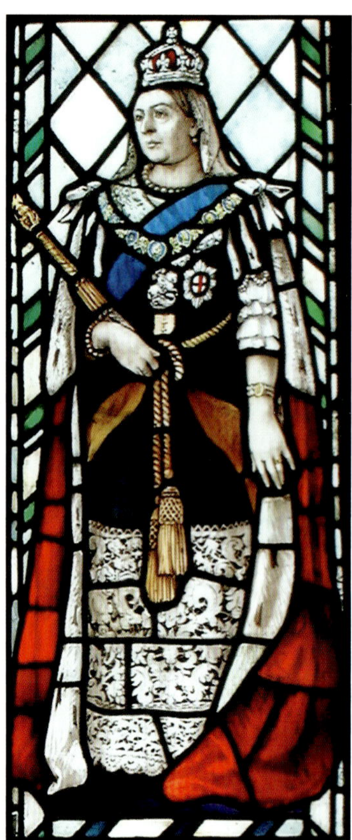

**THE FINDING OF CHRIST
THE SAVIOUR IN THE TEMPLE** 1910
Designed by Mary Lowndes
(1857–1929) after a painting by
William Holman Hunt (1827–1910);
made by Lowndes & Drury

This window is a close copy in glass
of the famous Pre-Raphaelite painting
of the same name by William Holman
Hunt, now in the Birmingham
Museum & Art Gallery. It was made
for a church in Oxford which, after
becoming redundant, was converted
for use as a library for Lincoln College
in the 1970s.

*From All Saints Church, Oxford. Donated
by Lincoln College, Oxford, 1974.* (1974.1.1)

QUEEN VICTORIA 1910
Designed and made by Hugh Arnold
(1872–1915)

During Queen Victoria's long reign
stained glass enjoyed a period of
enormous popularity and underwent
a technical and artistic transformation.
Many windows commemorating the
queen were produced in this period.

Hugh Arnold attended the Slade
School of Art in the 1890s and
subsequently the Central School of
Arts and Crafts, where he was a pupil
of Christopher Whall. His influential
*Stained Glass of the Middle Ages in
England and France* was published
in 1913. He was killed in action at
Gallipoli in 1915.

*From the church of St Mary Magdalene,
Bear Street, Barnstaple, Devon. Donated
by the London Stained Glass Repository,
1989.* (1989.5.1)

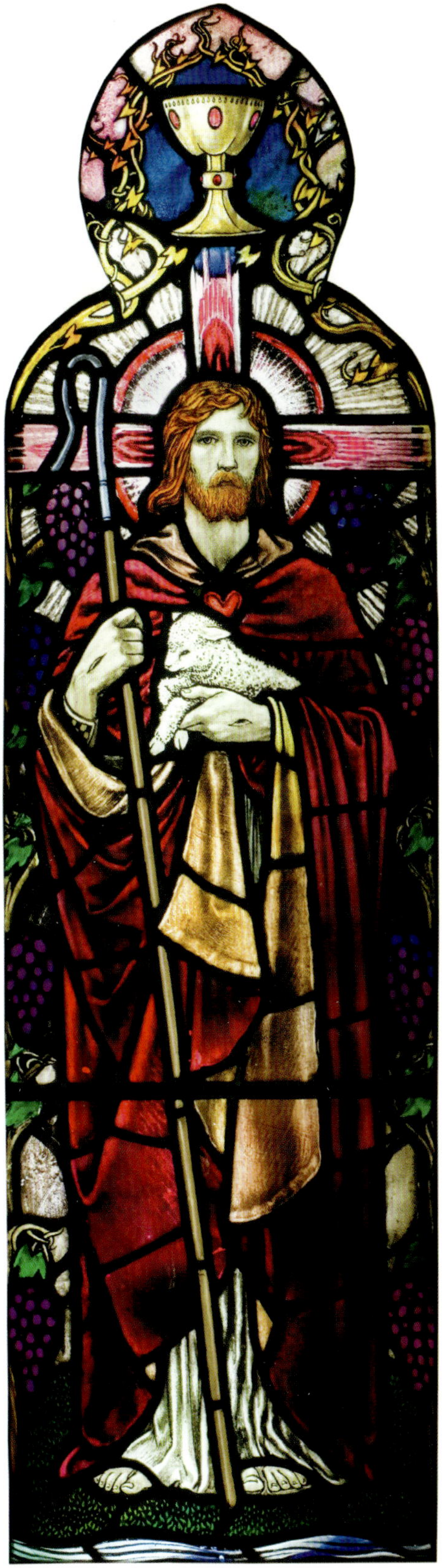

LEFT
CHRIST THE GOOD SHEPHERD 1913
Designed and made by Karl Parsons (1884–1934)

At the age of 15 Parsons became a pupil-apprentice of Christopher Whall. He later taught at both the Royal College of Art and the Central School of Arts and Crafts, and between 1908 and 1930 he had a studio in the Glass House. Here Parsons makes effective use of the sumptuous gold-pink slab glass of which he was so fond. Made by the addition of gold dust to the molten glass mix, it was one of the most expensive colours available.

From the church of St Michael, Sulhamstead, Berkshire. Donated by the Diocese of Oxford, 1977. (1977.3.2)

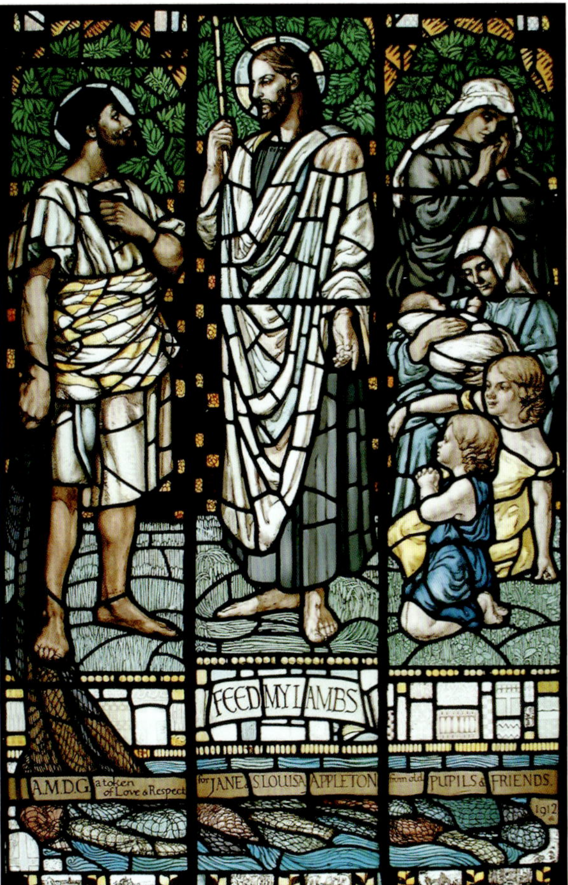

ABOVE
APPLETON MEMORIAL WINDOW: FEED MY LAMBS 1912
Designed and made by Margaret Chilton (1875–1962)

St Peter, the first apostle to whom the risen Christ appeared, was entrusted with the care of the Christian community, as depicted here.

Margaret Chilton trained at the Royal College of Art and studied stained glass under Christopher Whall, whose influence can be seen in the leadwork and decorative motifs used in this window. Most of her stained glass is to be found in Scotland, although there are also examples in England, Canada and New Zealand.

From the church of St John, Clifton, Bristol. Donated by Robert Mills Ltd, 1993. (1992.1)

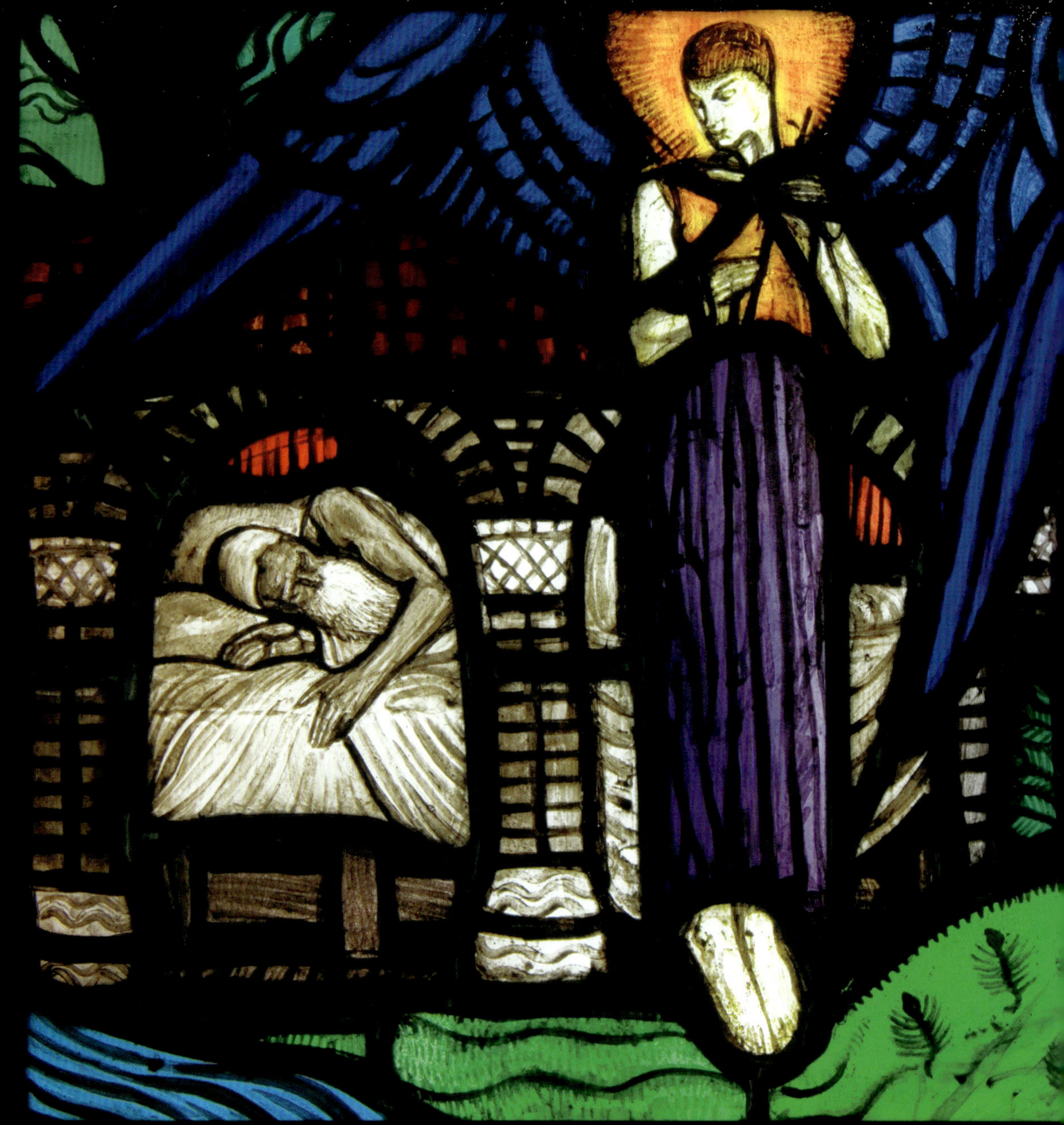

ST JOSEPH AND THE ANGEL 1920
Designed and made by Wilhelmina Geddes (1887–1955)

Wilhelmina Geddes was raised in Belfast, and in 1912 joined the Dublin Arts and Crafts stained glass co-operative An Túr Gloine (The Tower of Glass). Founded in 1903, this was the centre of Ireland's 20th-century stained glass revival, and Geddes's precocious talent flourished there. From 1925 she worked independently at the Glass House, designing windows, book illustrations, embroidered panels and linocut prints. Her expressive, angular, attenuated figural style can be seen in this panel showing an angel appearing to Joseph in a dream. Her attention to detail and exacting personal standards meant that her output was relatively small. Nonetheless, she undertook important commissions in Belgium, Canada, New Zealand and France as well as Great Britain and Ireland, and is one of the most widely admired stained glass artists of the 20th century.

From the artist's collection. Donated by Elizabeth Kerr, the artist's niece, 2001. (2001.3)

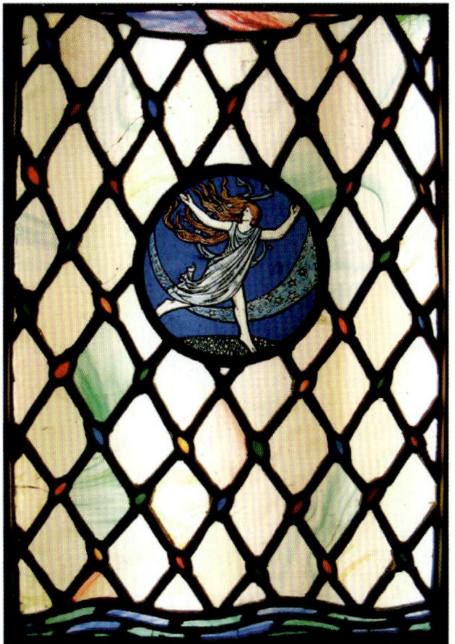

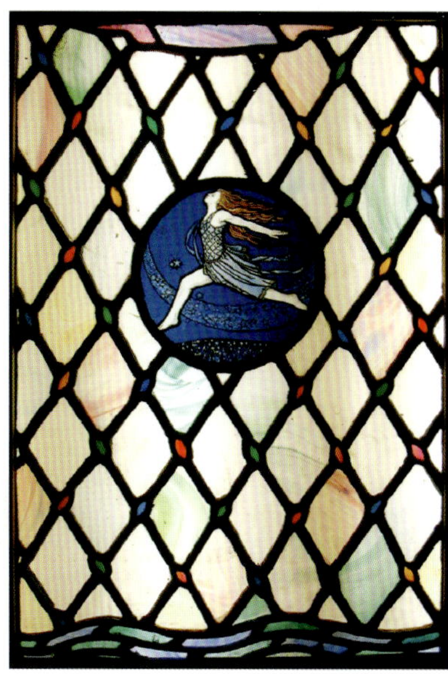

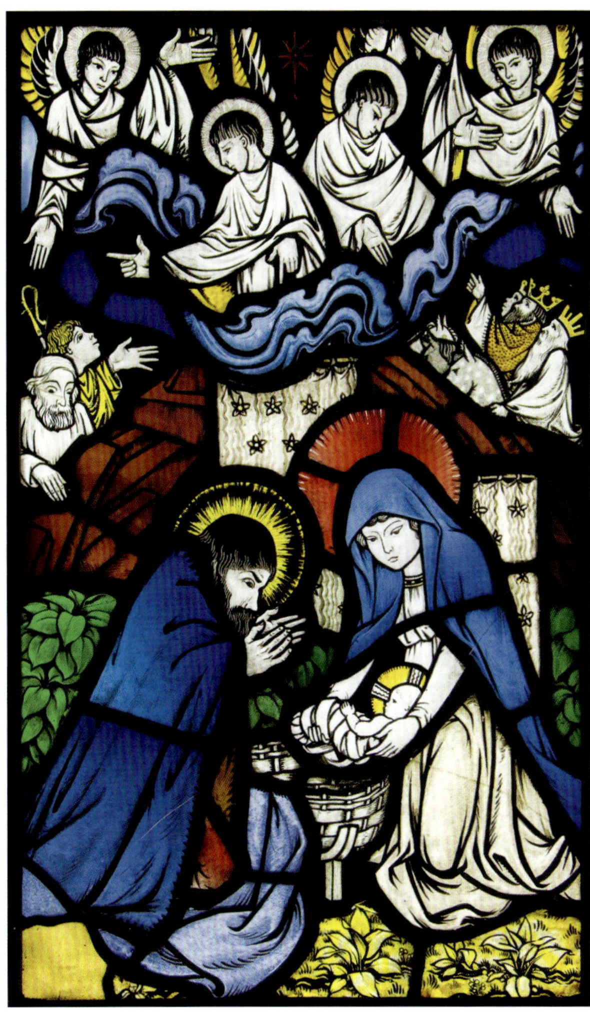

NATIVITY 1923

Designed and made by Francis Spear
(1902–79)

In this tender scene the excitement of
parenthood is shown as Mary and Joseph
gather around the newborn Christ Child.
Joseph extends his arms to the infant while
Mary looks on contemplatively. The panel
illustrates the three main events of the
Nativity in one scene. A group of robed
angels are shown amongst the clouds
above. Some of the angels point to two
shepherds watching the scene on the left,
while the others direct our attention to the
Magi following the star on the right.

Spear studied under Karl Parsons before
becoming pupil assistant to stained glass
artist and teacher Martin Travers. This panel
was probably fired at the Glass House,
where Travers had a studio.

From the artist's studio. Donated by Simon
Spear, 2012. (2012.4)

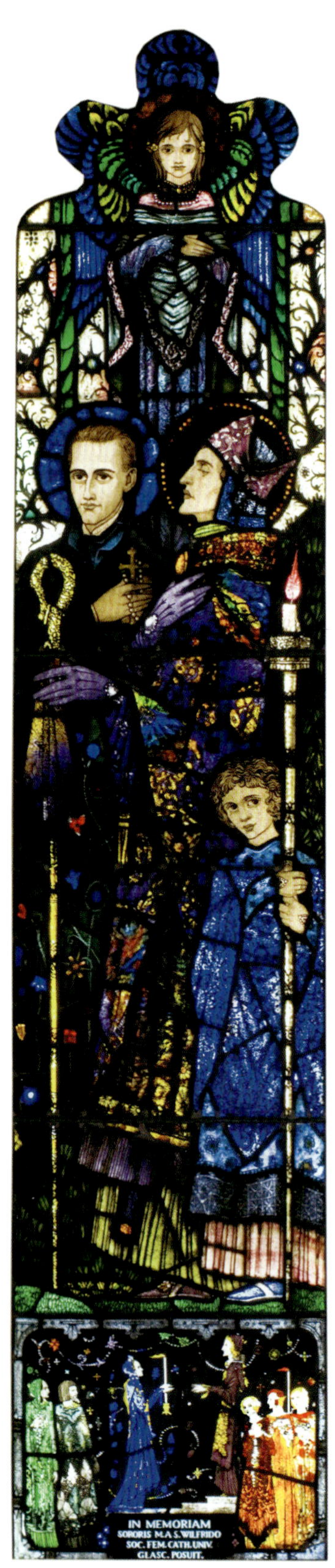

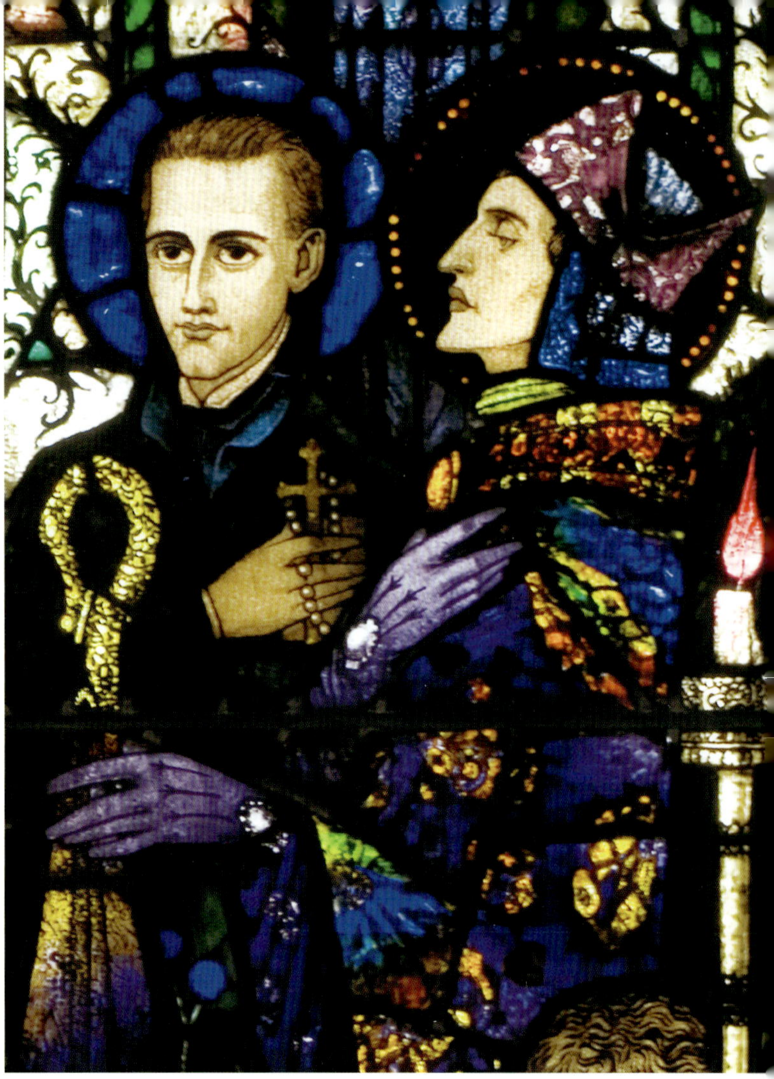

ST WILFRID AND ST JOHN BERCHMANS AND THE PRESENTATION OF OUR LADY IN THE TEMPLE 1927
Designed and made by Harry Clarke (1889–1931)

This tall lancet depicts the figures of St Wilfrid (died 709), the aristocratic Bishop of York, and St John Berchmans (1599–1621), a Belgian Jesuit noted for his scholarship and piety. In the lower panel is a small scene showing the Presentation of the Virgin Mary in the Temple. These saints and subjects were chosen to commemorate two successive College Principals at the Convent of Notre Dame, the first Catholic female training college in Scotland. Sister Mary Wilfrid commissioned the first set of stained glass windows for the Convent Chapel from Harry Clarke as war memorials, but they were delayed and she died before they were completed. This was one of two windows devoted to her, donated by Glasgow University Catholic Women's Association. The design was altered after the sudden death of Sister Mary to include St John Berchmans.

Dublin-born Harry Clarke inherited a family stained glass and church decorating business, and played a major role in the Arts and Crafts movement in Ireland. Renowned as a book illustrator as well as a stained glass artist, he was a craftsman of unequalled talent, creating jewel-like effects by the use of extensive plating and acid-etching.

From the Lady Chapel, Convent of Notre Dame, Dowanhill, Glasgow. Purchased with help from The Art Fund, The ACE/ V&A Purchase Grant Fund and Phillida Shaw, 1998. (1998.2)

ST CHRISTOPHER 1928
Designed and made by Leonard Potter (1903–62)

Leonard Potter trained under Karl Parsons at the Central School of Arts and Crafts and later became his assistant at the Glass House, contributing to many of his windows between 1925 and 1930. Potter was also a friend of Harry Clarke, whom he assisted in the latter years of his life. Although talented, Potter appears to have attracted only one commission for stained glass outside his family, for a window of Christ teaching Mary, sister of Martha, for All Saints Church, Monkwearmouth, in 1929. This panel depicting St Christopher, the Christ-bearer, made the previous year, may have served as an example of his work, or as practice. He reluctantly abandoned a career in stained glass shortly afterwards, becoming an artist designer in the BBC publicity department. In later life he also produced linocuts, engravings, drawings and paintings, and designed and made silver jewellery and woven rugs.

From the artist's studio. Donated by the artist's family, 2016.
(2016.8)

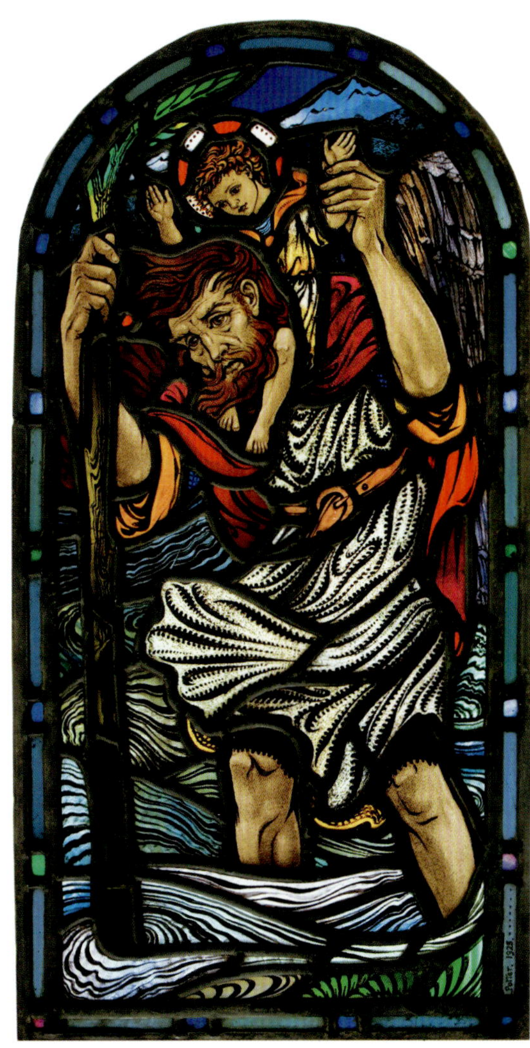

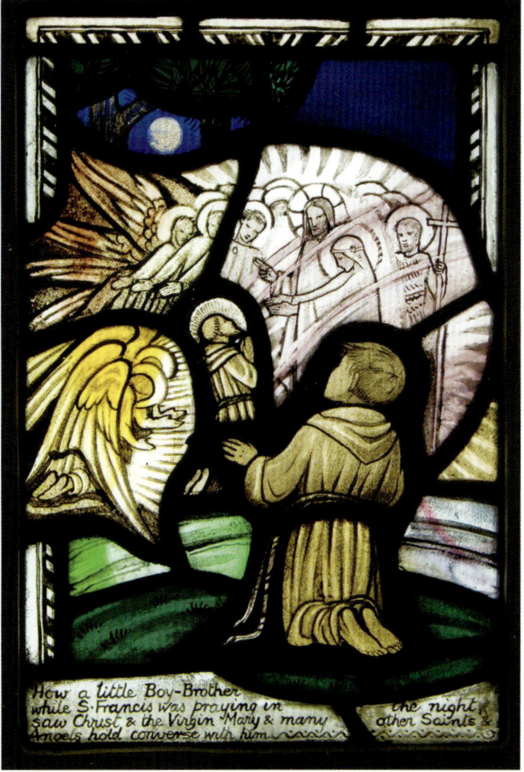

FRANCISCAN BOY AND A VISION OF HEAVEN 1931
Designed and made by Margaret Edith Aldrich Rope
(1891–1988)

St Francis of Assisi founded the Franciscan Order in 1210. The order, whose members believed in absolute poverty, became popular in Europe and arrived in England in 1224.

Margaret E.A. Rope attended the Chelsea School of Art and later the Central School of Arts and Crafts, where she studied under Karl Parsons and Alfred Drury. She also worked with her cousin Margaret Agnes Rope at the Glass House, and after 1945 had her own studio, assisted by her friend and pupil Claire Dawson. Her maker's mark, a tortoise, refers to her family nickname, 'Tor'.

Original location unknown. Donated by Mary Nottingham, 1990.
(1990.8a)

INTO THE 20TH CENTURY

Alongside the more independent and innovative productions of the emerging Arts and Crafts movement, a number of large commercial studios continued to provide employment for artists and craftsmen in the late 19th century. The firms of C.E. Kempe & Co., founded in 1869, and Burlison & Grylls, founded in 1868, championed a lighter, highly refined and decorative version of late Gothic style, which was influenced by the more linear styles of late medieval German and Netherlandish stained glass.

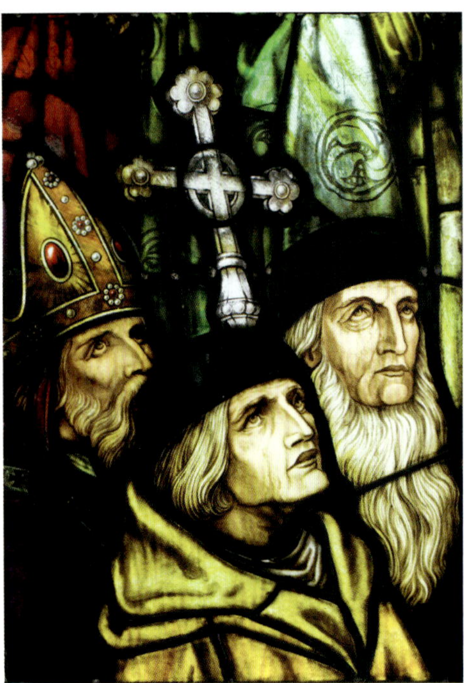

In Britain traditional styles continued to pervade stained glass design well into the 20th century. Architect Sir J. Ninian Comper, who trained in the studio of stained glass and decorative artist Charles Eamer Kempe and the architectural firm Bodley & Garner, was an important influence. Both Comper and his former assistant Martin Travers were associated with the Anglo-Catholic movement and shared a preference for late medieval and renaissance styles and the extensive use of white glass with delicate application of paint and silver stain, which made for lighter, brighter church interiors. Christopher Webb, another of Comper's former assistants, was a skilled draughtsman who developed his own distinct style characterised by strong lines and delicate modelling. These artists represented a more refined yet traditional style of stained glass that continued to be popular in the inter-war period.

FATHERS OF THE CHURCH 1904
Designed by Henry Gustave Hiller (1864–1946); made by Reuben Bennett (active 1900–10)

This panel is from an east window depicting Christ in Glory with angels, saints and Church Fathers. The window is an unusual composition uniting five lights. At almost 9m high and over 3m wide, the entire window was rescued before the church was demolished in the 1980s.

Henry Gustave Hiller's bold design was interpreted by Reuben Bennett using layers of thick, streaky glass, to spectacular effect. Bennett had a studio in the Manchester area and his work exemplified a commercial response to the ideals of the Arts and Crafts movement.

From the Church of St Paul, New Cross, Manchester. Donated by the Manchester Diocese, 1982. (1982.16.4)

OPPOSITE, DETAIL
THE FACE OF MY FATHER 1892
Designed by John William Brown (1842–1928); made by James Powell & Sons

One hundred panels of stained glass were removed from this large London church before it was demolished. This classically draped figure in a sentimental Victorian pose has been painted using a variety of brushes on a beautifully muted glass. J.W. Brown was a painter of portraits and genre scenes as well as a stained glass designer. He joined James Powell & Sons in 1877, eventually becoming its principal in-house designer. His most notable works are the east windows of the Cathedral of St John the Divine, New York City, and Liverpool Anglican Cathedral.

From Christ Church, Lancaster Gate, London W2. Donated by the Diocese of London, 1978. (1978.6)

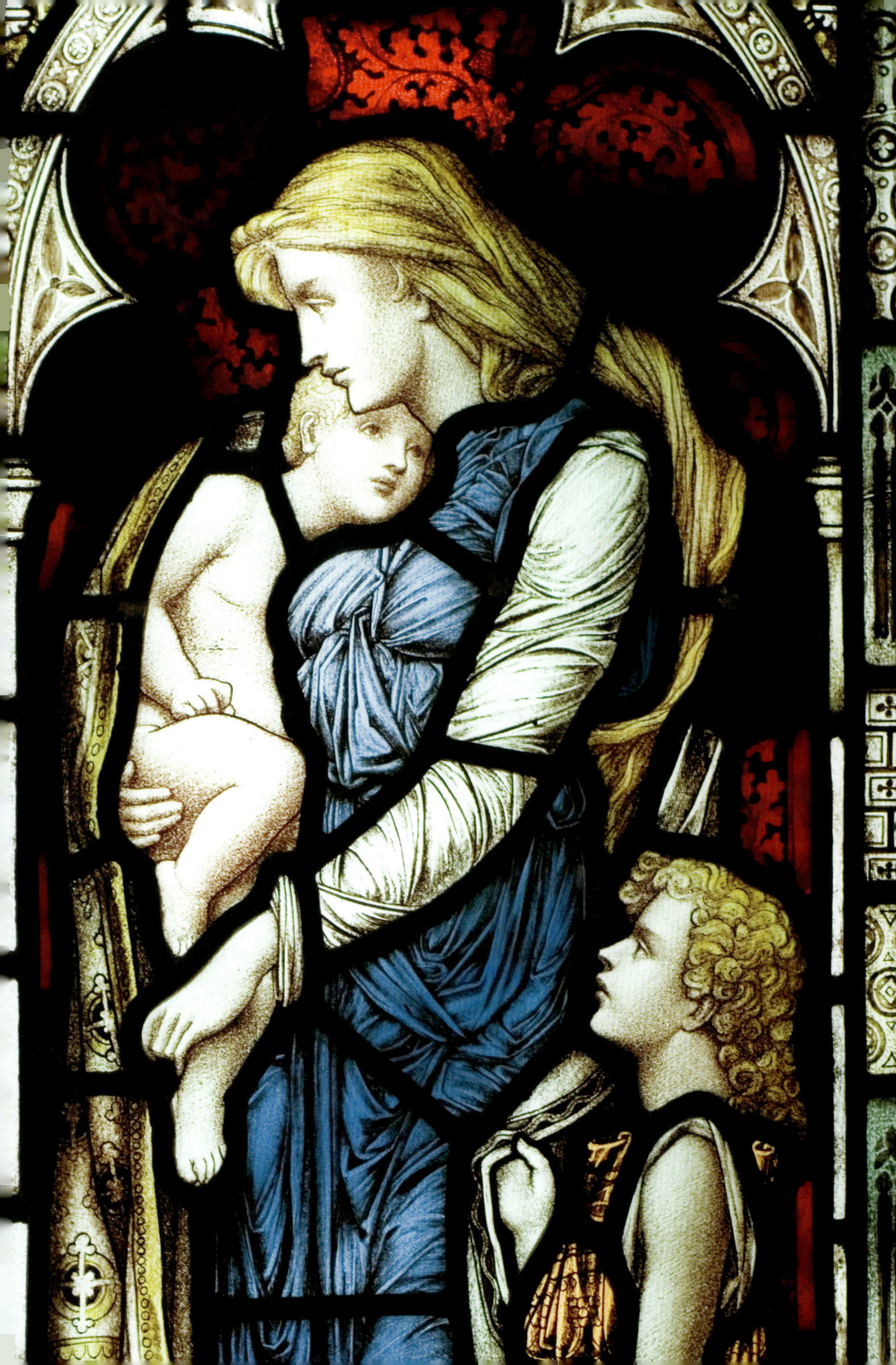

THE MAY QUEEN 1900

Designed by George Parlby (1856 –1944);
made by Thomas Cowell

A traditional English May Queen, crowned with
flowers and robed in a white gown is the subject of
this small, delicately painted panel.

George Parlby designed for many stained glass
studios, including Curtis, Ward & Hughes and James
Powell & Sons, and also worked independently
during the first half of the 20th century. Known for
his Bohemian manner and style of dress, he was a
member of the Worshipful Company of Glaziers and
became Master of the Art Workers Guild in 1942.
Thomas Cowell, who made this window, was the
principal glass painter for James Powell & Sons.

*From the studio of Thomas Cowell. Donated by
John Wilson, 1992.* (1992.4.8)

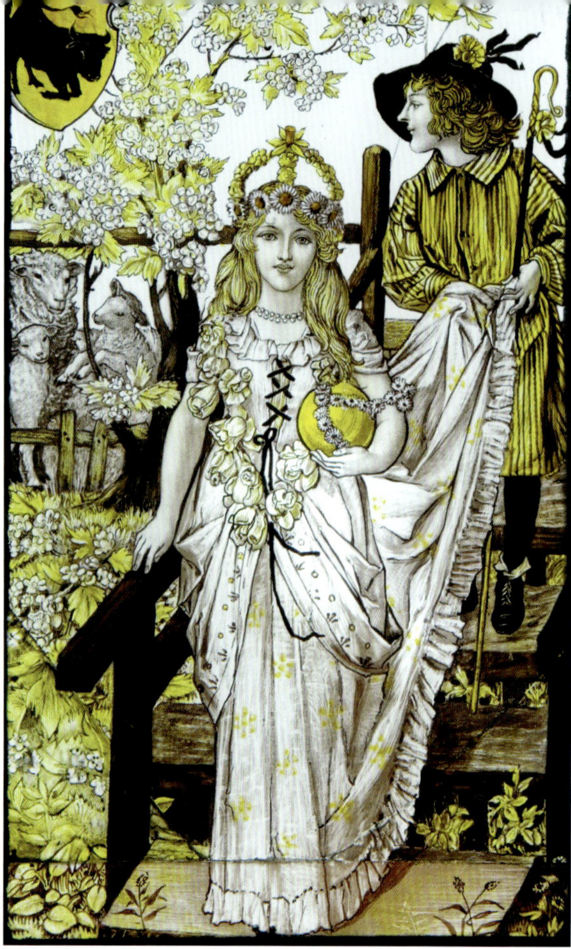

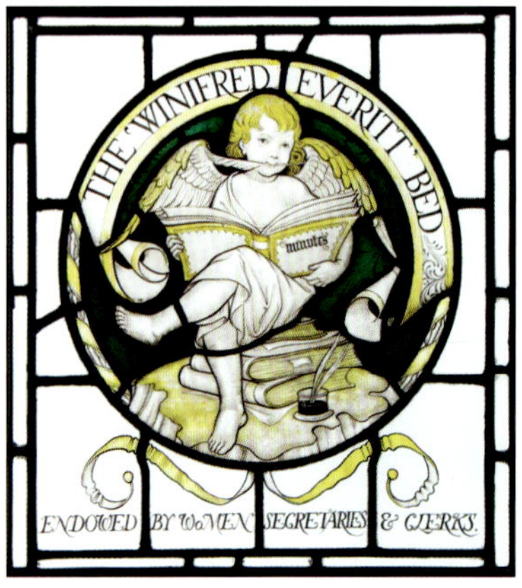

CHERUB SCRIBE *c.*1920–30

Designed and made by
Christopher Webb (1886 –1966)

The Elizabeth Garrett Anderson
Hospital for women, founded in
1872, bears the name of Britain's first
woman to qualify as a doctor. Above
each bed was a stained glass panel
designed and made by Christopher
Webb, sponsored by different groups
and societies.

Webb trained with J. Ninian
Comper and shared with him a
preference for late medieval and
renaissance styles, with a pale palette
and lightly modelled painting. These
panels are examples of Webb's finest
early work.

*From the Elizabeth Garrett Anderson
Hospital, London WC1. Donated by the
Elizabeth Garrett Anderson Hospital
Appeal Trust, 1996.* (1992.10.2)

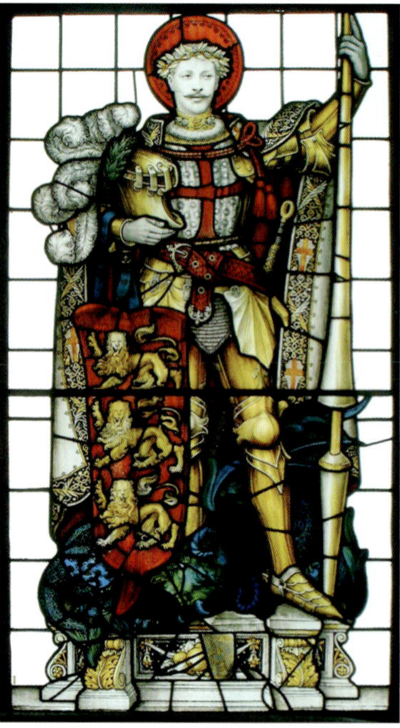

THE DUKE OF CLARENCE AS ST GEORGE 1905

Designed by John Lisle (1870 –1927);
made by C.E. Kempe & Co.

Queen Alexandra commissioned
the window from which this panel
comes in memory of her eldest son,
Albert Victor, Duke of Clarence. The
Duke, who died in 1892 at the age
of 28, is depicted in the guise of
St George, patron saint of England.
The window was damaged during
an air raid in 1940.

Charles Eamer Kempe began his
artistic career as a church decorator.
Inspired by the styles of the 15th
and early 16th centuries, his firm
became one of the most successful
and prolific of the later 19th century,
with a highly distinctive studio style.
The studio closed in 1934.

Lent by Her Majesty The Queen, 1984.
(L1984.11.1)

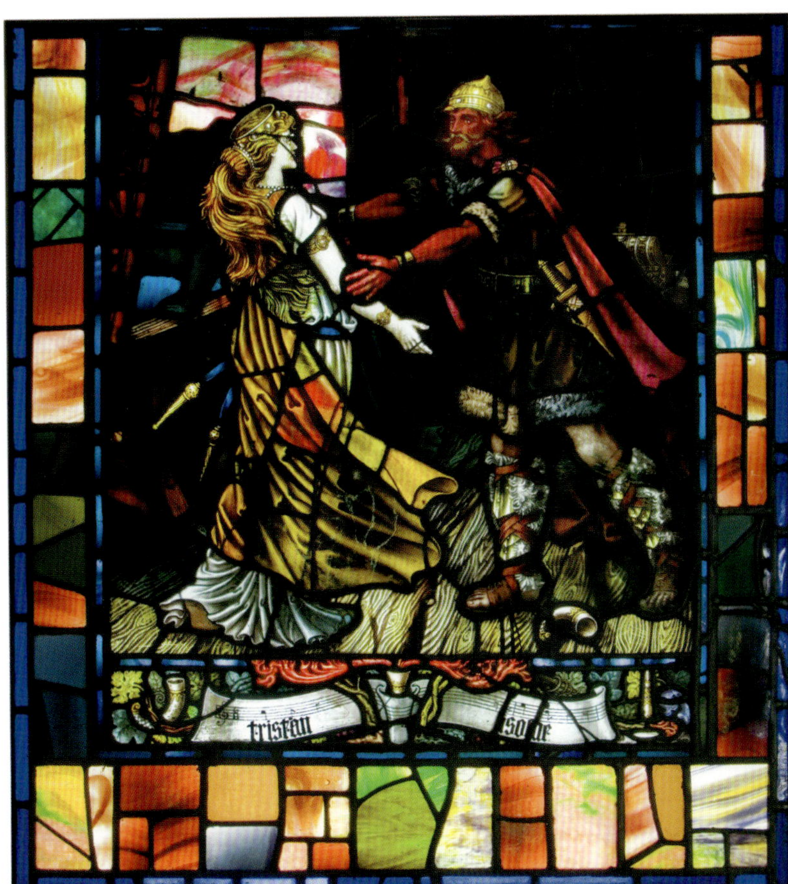

TRISTAN AND ISOLDE *c.*1900

Designed and made by
James Silvester Sparrow
(1862–1929)

This panel, full of movement
and dramatic gesture,
depicts an episode from the
Cornish legend of Tristan
and Isolde. Set in the time
of King Arthur, this medieval
romance involves a tragic
love triangle between Tristan,
his uncle King Mark of
Cornwall and Isolde, his
uncle's wife. In this scene
Tristan and Isolde are in
an ecstasy of love after
mistakenly drinking a love
potion from the horn cup at
Tristan's feet.

J.S. Sparrow, who referred
to himself as 'the Wagner
of stained glass', achieved
dramatic effects by *plating*
or layering glass of different
colours and textures in the
same very wide leads.

*Made for the London apartment
of Miss Horniman, whose family
established the Horniman
Museum, London. On loan from
Neil Phillips, 2001.* (L2001.5)

MORNING 1932

Designed and made by Ervin Bossanyi (1891–1975)

Born in Southern Hungary, Bossanyi studied in
Budapest, Perugia, Rome, Paris and London
before the First World War. In 1919 he settled in
Germany, relocating from Lübeck to Hamburg
in 1929. Anticipating the persecution of the Nazi
regime that claimed the lives of some of his family,
he emigrated to England in 1934. *Morning* and its
companion panel, *Evening* were among the last
works he made before he left Germany. Bossanyi
was a versatile designer and prolific painter who
worked in many media – sculpture, metalwork,
and ceramics. But he is perhaps best known for his
work in stained glass, with windows in Canterbury
and Washington cathedrals, the New West End
Synagogue and Tate Britain, London. Miraculously,
the original windows, of which these panels are
replicas, survived the bombing of Hamburg during
the Second World War.

*Replicas, with some details changed, of windows made for
the Volkshochschule, Vetersen, near Hamburg. From the
artist's collection. Donated by Jo Bossanyi, 1983.* (1983.1)

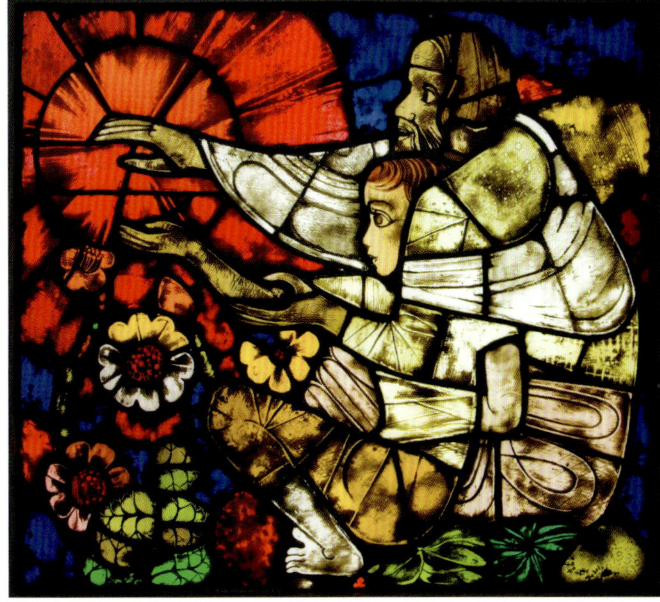

THE POST-WAR PERIOD

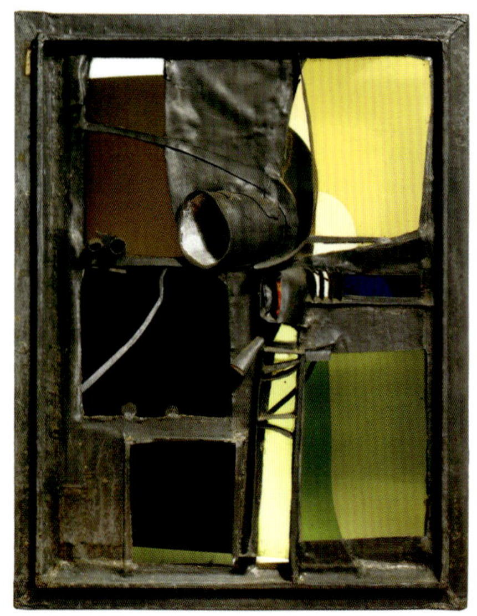

The tragedies of two World Wars created an enormous demand for memorial windows in Britain. This work occupied many of the large studios established in the Victorian period well into the 1940s and 1950s. Alongside more traditional figurative stained glass, after the Second World War modern stained glass reached its zenith. Artists of the stature of Georges Braque, Henri Matisse and Marc Chagall in Europe and John Piper in Britain were influenced by modern abstract and expressionist art and adopted new approaches to designing stained glass, working in tandem with skilled craftsmen.

The glazing of the new Coventry Cathedral, rebuilt to the designs of architect Sir Basil Spence in 1956–62 after wartime bombing left the old Cathedral a ruin, was highly significant for British stained glass. Dramatic windows by John Piper and Patrick Reyntiens, Lawrence Lee, Keith New, Geoffrey Clarke and Margaret Traherne demonstrated the beauty and power of abstract and non-figurative designs. This new generation of artists experimented with new materials as well as styles. The *dalle-de-verre* technique of using pieces of coloured slab glass set in a matrix of concrete or epoxy resin developed in France in the 1930s and became popular in Britain in the 1950s and 1960s. In modern buildings it was used to glaze large windows and sometimes entire walls, and thus had an important structural as well as decorative role.

FRAGMENT 1956

Designed and made by Geoffrey Clarke (1924–2014)

Clarke combined his skills as sculptor and glass artist to make this three-dimensional abstract relief artwork. The metal frame was cast from an impression in sand and then coated in lead. Sheets of lead, bent into tubular shapes, protrude from the front and back. The inside of the central tube is coated with aluminium leaf, into which is set a jewel-like piece of yellow-orange slab glass. These sculptural aspects provide a contrast with the flat pieces of coloured sheet glass, held in place by strips of lead sheet.

Fragment was created as a focal artwork for *Flat '56*, an exhibition of wallpapers and fabrics organised by Sir Hugh Casson in 1956.

From the artist's studio. Purchased with support from The Art Fund, The ACE/V&A Purchase Grant Fund and The Geoffrey Clarke Appeal, 2015. (2014.2)

OPPOSITE, DETAIL

ABSTRACT PANEL *c.*1956–9

Designed by John Piper (1903–92);
made by Patrick Reyntiens (born 1925)

John Piper was an established painter, printmaker and stage designer before designing his first stained glass at the age of 48. His colour designs were translated into stained glass by master craftsman Patrick Reyntiens. This abstract panel appears to have been created as a trial panel or experimental piece around the time when Piper and Reyntiens were engaged on major projects at Coventry Cathedral and the London headquarters of decorative designers and manufacturers Arthur Sanderson & Son (now Sanderson Hotel). It was shown in *British Artist Craftsmen: An Exhibition of Contemporary Work* that toured the USA in 1959–60 and Piper then gave it to his friend the architect (Margaret) Justin Blanco White to thank her for redesigning his studio.

From the artist's studio. On loan from Dusa McDuff, 2003.
(L2003.8)

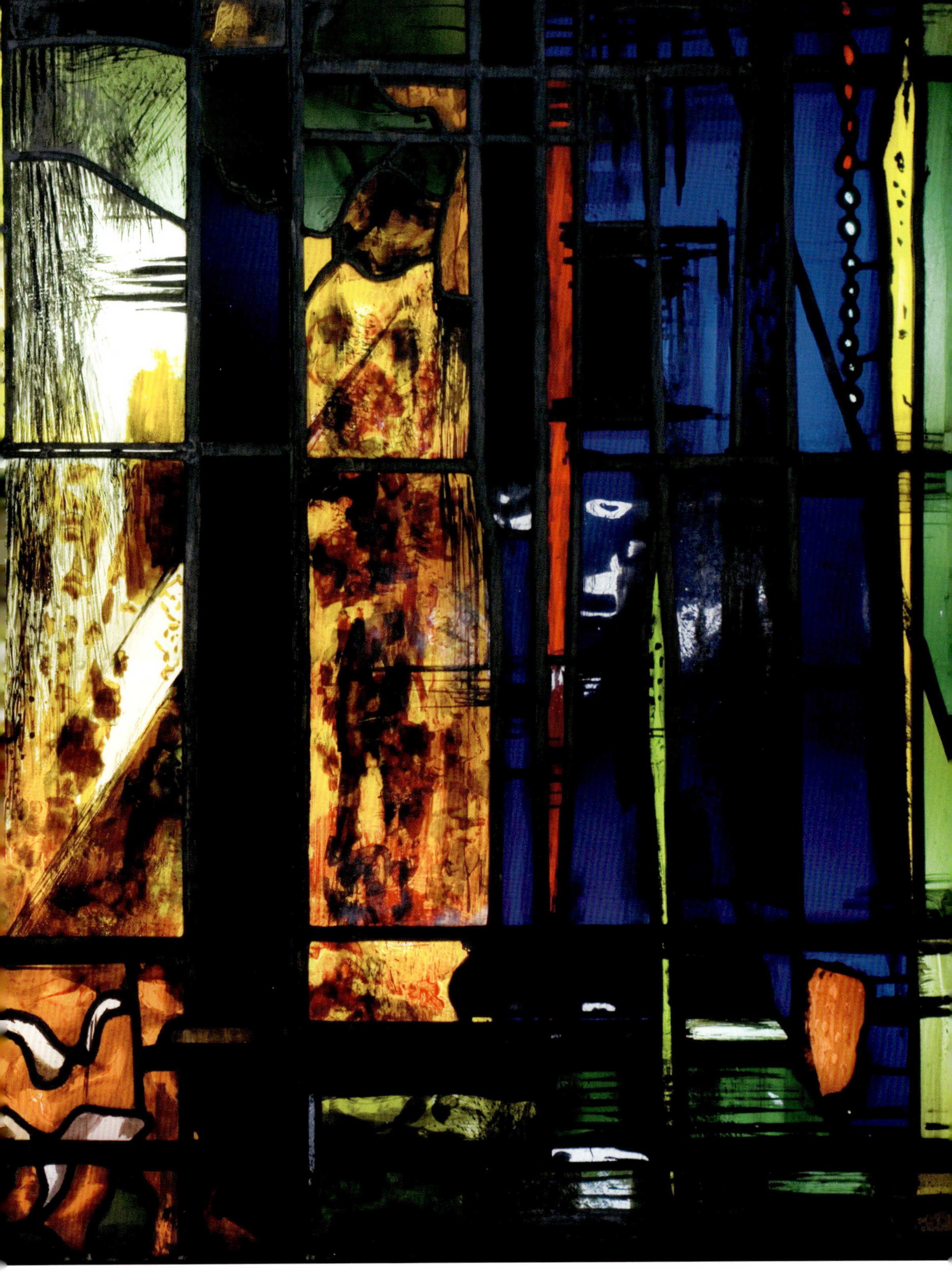

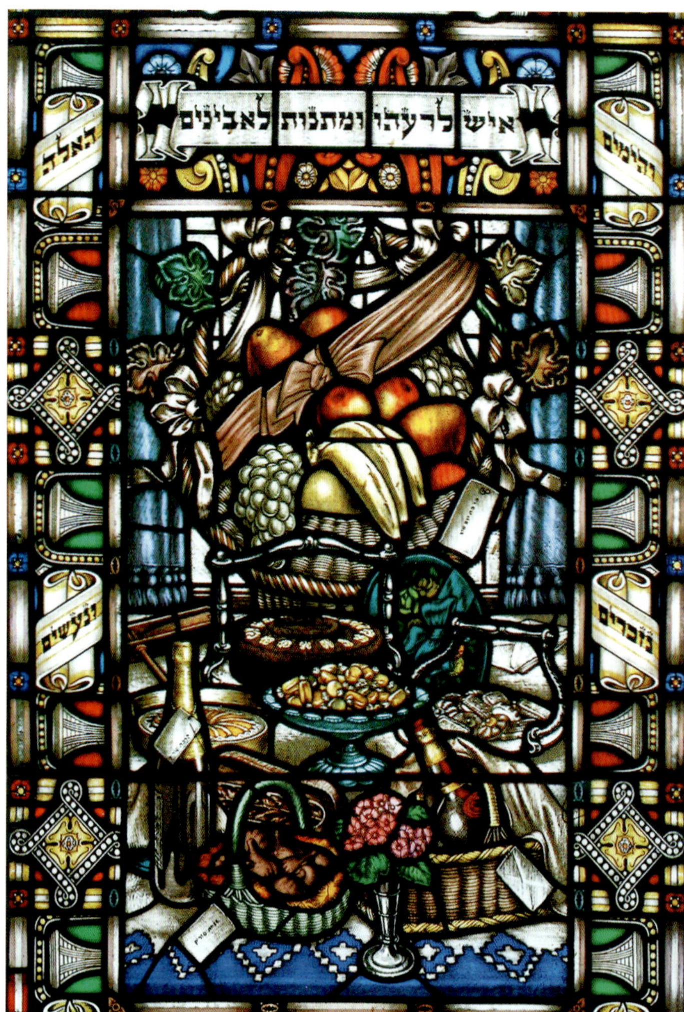

LEFT, DETAIL
THE FESTIVAL OF PURIM 1954
Designed and made by David Hillman
(1894–1974)

The Jewish festival of Purim celebrates events described in the Old Testament in which Esther, a Jewish girl (later Queen to King Exerxes of Persia), prevents a plan to slaughter the Jews living in Persia. Esther's bravery is commemorated with great revelry: here we see a lavish array of food and drink accompanied by Hebrew inscriptions.

David Hillman arrived in Glasgow from Russia with his parents and sister in 1908, when his father was appointed Rabbi of Glasgow. Hillman gained a scholarship at the Glasgow School of Art before training at the Royal Academy of Arts, and began creating stained glass in the early 1930s. Hillman made 16 windows celebrating festivals for the Bayswater Ashkenazi-Orthodox Synagogue in Chichester Place, Paddington, in the 1950s, many of which were relocated to Borehamwood Synagogue in 1965, when the Bayswater building was demolished.

From the Bayswater Ashkenazi-Orthodox Synagogue, Paddington, London W2. Donated by the London Stained Glass Repository, 2007. (2007.1)

CHRIST MEETING HIS MOTHER *c.*1950
Designed and made by Evie Hone (1894–1955)

Evie Hone was born in Dublin into a family long associated with the arts in Ireland. After training in London she went to Paris in 1920, where she studied Cubist painting. In 1935 she converted to Roman Catholicism, joined the Dublin Arts and Crafts stained glass co-operative An Túr Gloine (the Tower of Glass) and later opened her own studio. Her work was influenced by her faith, her passion for medieval Irish sculpture and her admiration for the artist Georges Rouault.

This panel was one of a series depicting the Stations of the Cross. Although severely handicapped by infantile paralysis, Hone did not allow her disability to deter her from her career as an artist. At the end of her life she continued to make windows from her wheelchair.

From the artist's collection. Donated by Kay Richmond and Dorothy Charlton, 1989. (1989.3)

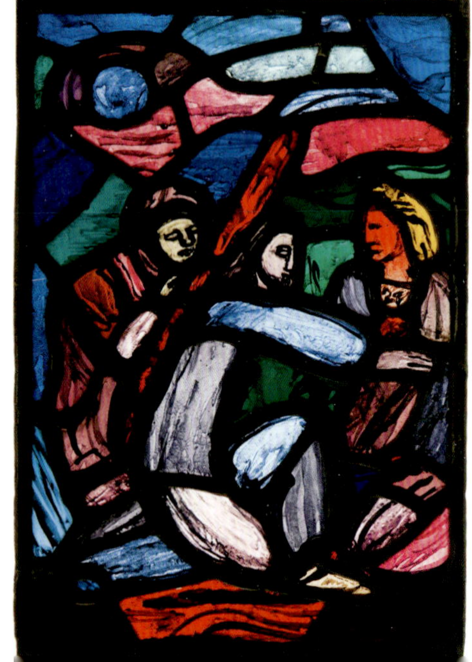

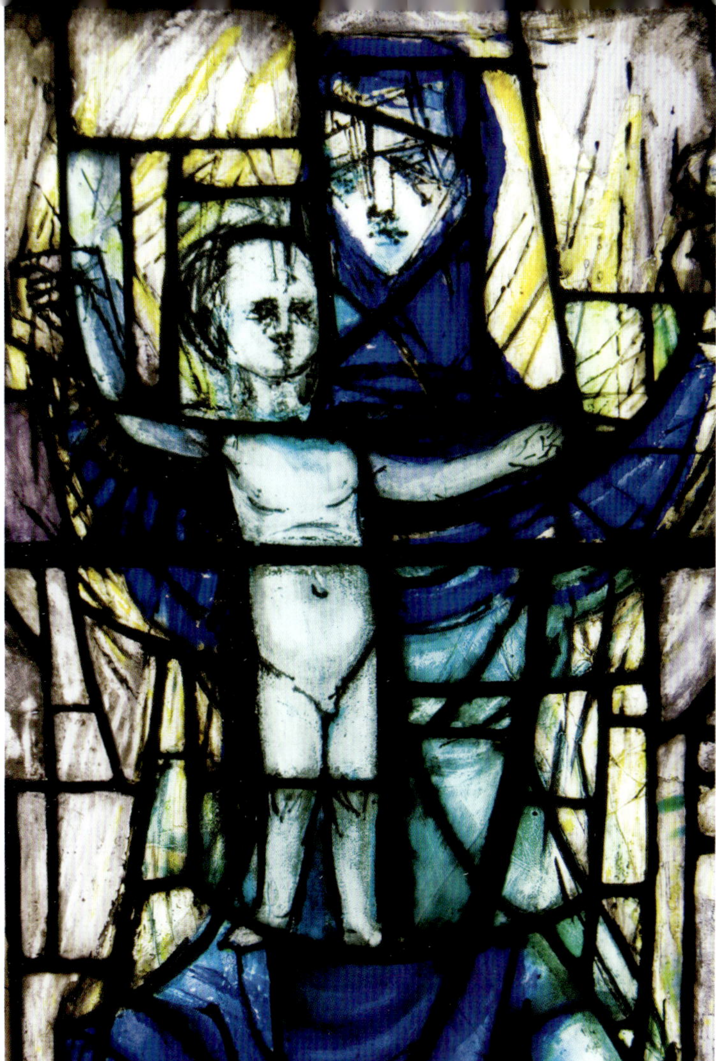

VIRGIN AND CHRIST CHILD 1956

Designed and made by
Margaret Traherne (1919–2006)

Margaret Traherne studied at the
Royal College of Art in 1945–8 under
Lawrence Lee and Martin Travers,
who encouraged her interest in
stained glass. This panel was one of
her earliest works in stained glass,
made for a priory church in Sussex.
The expressive painting style and use
of blue flashed glass, which has been
acid-etched to re veal the white glass
underneath, reveals the influence of
French expressionism on her early
stained glass.

*From Michelham Priory, Upper Dicker,
Hailsham, Sussex. Donated by the artist,
2005.* (2005.2)

SIREN 1958–62

Designed and made by Pauline Boty (1938–66)

The only female painter in the British Pop art
movement, Pauline Boty joined the stained glass
department at the Royal College of Art in 1958.
Most of her artistic output, however, were paintings
and collages in her unique Pop-art style.

This stained glass panel, like much of Boty's
work, celebrates female sexuality and challenges
gender inequality. The female figure, a siren, at
the centre of the panel appears as a phallic form.
The cave in the right background is based on the
16th-century cave doorway in the Italian garden
of Vicino Orsini, Duke of Bomarzo, and might be
interpreted as a vulvic image.

From the artist's studio. On loan from June Milne, 2009.
(L2009.4)

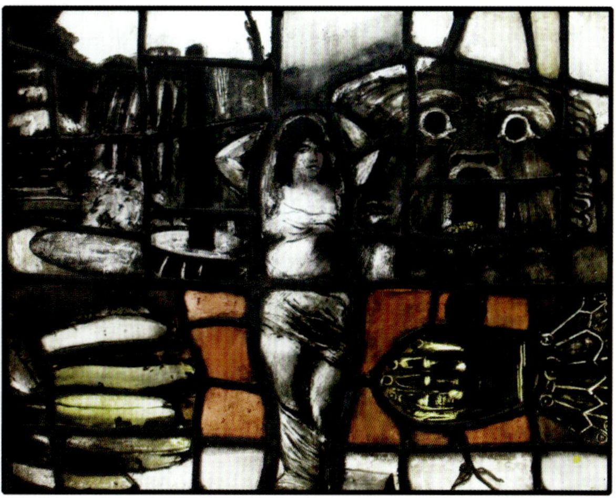

CHRIST THE WORKER 1978

Designed and made by Carl Edwards
(1914–85)

This panel is a replica of the head of Christ
from Carl Edwards's 16m-high great west
Benedicite window of Liverpool Anglican
Cathedral. It was made for an exhibition in
Chartres in 1978 and exemplifies the artist's
use of dramatic paint lines to reinforce the
imposing effect of the lead lines.

Edwards began working at Whitefriars
Glass at the age of 14 and became chief
designer on the death of James Hogan.
In 1952 he left Whitefriars to set up a
studio in London's Apothecaries' Hall in
partnership with Hugh Powell. In 1972 he
moved to the Glass House and took over
the firm of Lowndes & Drury.

*From the artist's studio. On loan from Caroline
Benyon, the artist's daughter, 1993.* (L1993.2)

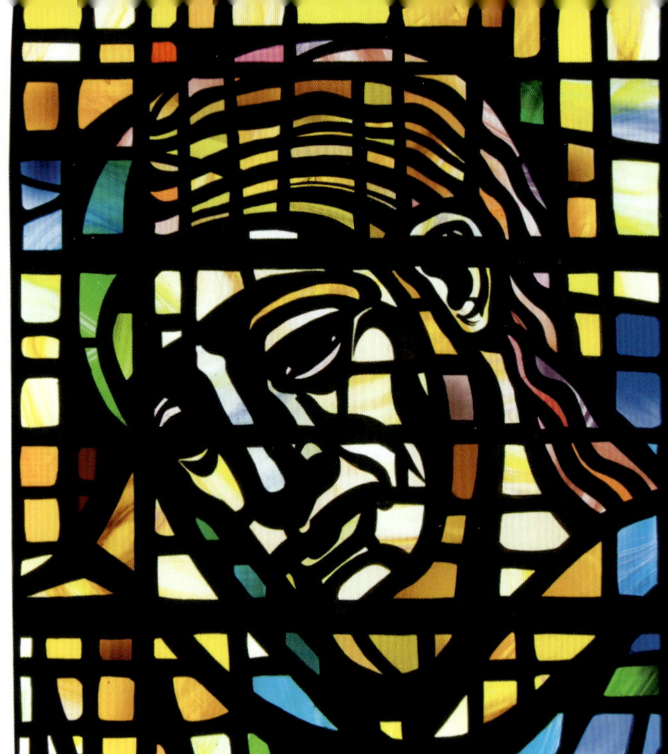

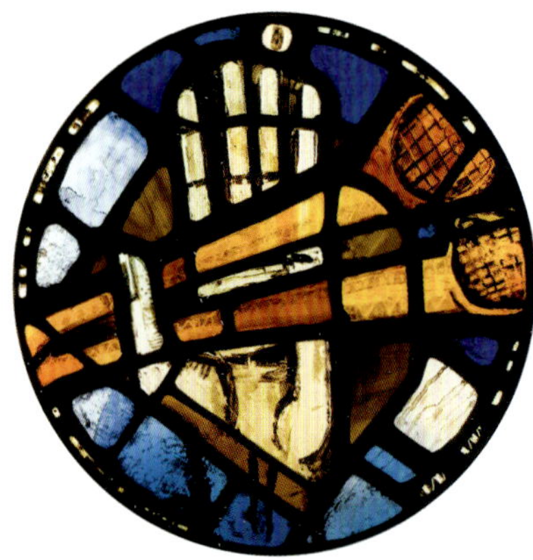

ABOVE, DETAIL

ROSE WINDOW 1960s

Designed and made by Alan Younger
(1933–2004)

After studying Fine Art at the Central School
of Arts and Crafts in London, Alan Younger
worked in the stained glass studios of Carl
Edwards and Lawrence Lee before he set up
his own studio in 1966. Among his many
notable commissions were the great rose
window of St Alban's Cathedral (1987)
and a window for the Henry VII Chapel in
Westminster Abbey (2000).

Made in the early part of his career, this
panel was part of a rose window, with eight
roundels depicting angels holding trumpets
and the Alpha and Omega symbols, with
a dove in the centre. According to the
recollections of Younger's family, the
window was executed as a 'labour of love'
for a church near his home.

*From St Paul's Church, Taymount Rise, London
SE2. Donated by Zoe Younger, 2008.* (2008.14.4)

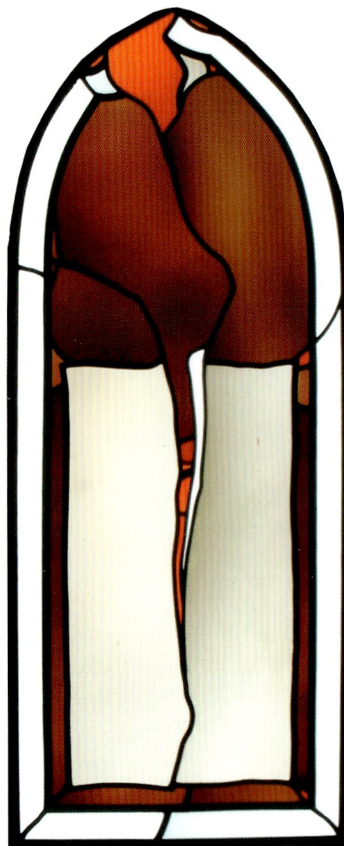

EVERLASTING LIFE 1978

Designed by Johannes
Schreiter (born 1930)

German post-war stained
glass, and in particular the
work of Johannes Schreiter,
has been highly influential
in Britain. Schreiter studied
drawing and painting first
at Münster, then Mainz and
Berlin. He took up a teaching
post at the Bremen Academy
of Art in 1960 before becoming
Professor at the School of
Decorative Arts in Frankfurt
between 1963 and 1988. In
this panel, characteristic of
Schreiter's work, no paint
has been used. The design,
symbolising everlasting life,
derives its effect from the
strong linear lead lines, colour
and quality of the glass.

*Replica panel of a window in
the church of St Laurentius,
Niederkalbach, Germany.
Donated by the artist, 1980.*
(1980.1)

DALLE-DE-VERRE PANEL 1962
Designed and made by
Margaret Traherne (1919–2006)

The *dalle-de-verre* technique, which
involved setting slabs of glass in
concrete or resin, was developed in
France in the early 20th century. It was
especially popular in modern buildings
after the Second World War. This
panel was part of an entire wall glazed
using this technique at the west end
of Westbourne Park Baptist Church,
London. The church was demolished in
2016. A few years before this panel was
made, in 1958, Traherne contributed a
whole scheme of *dalle-de-verre* windows,
each over 15m high, to the Chapel of
Unity in Coventry Cathedral.

*From Westbourne Park Baptist Church,
London W2. Donated by the Pastor and
congregation of Westbourne Park Baptist
Church, 2016.* (2016.13)

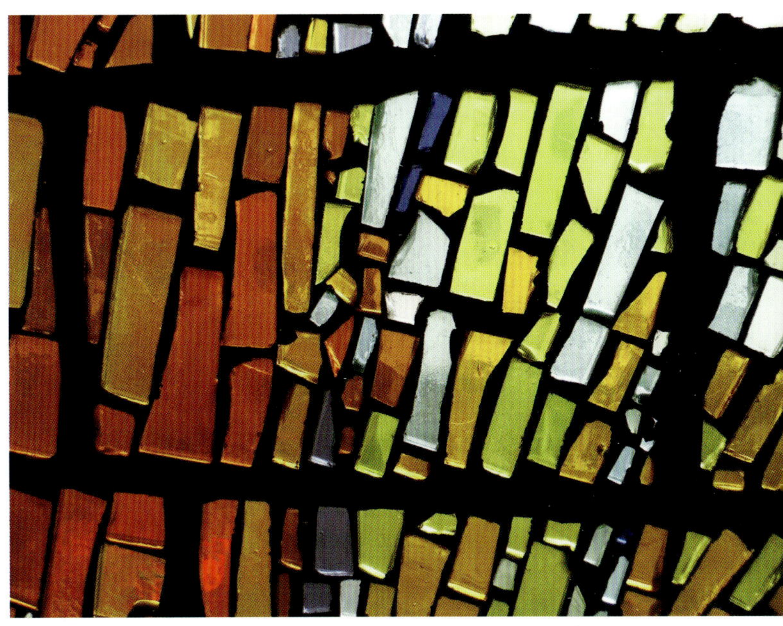

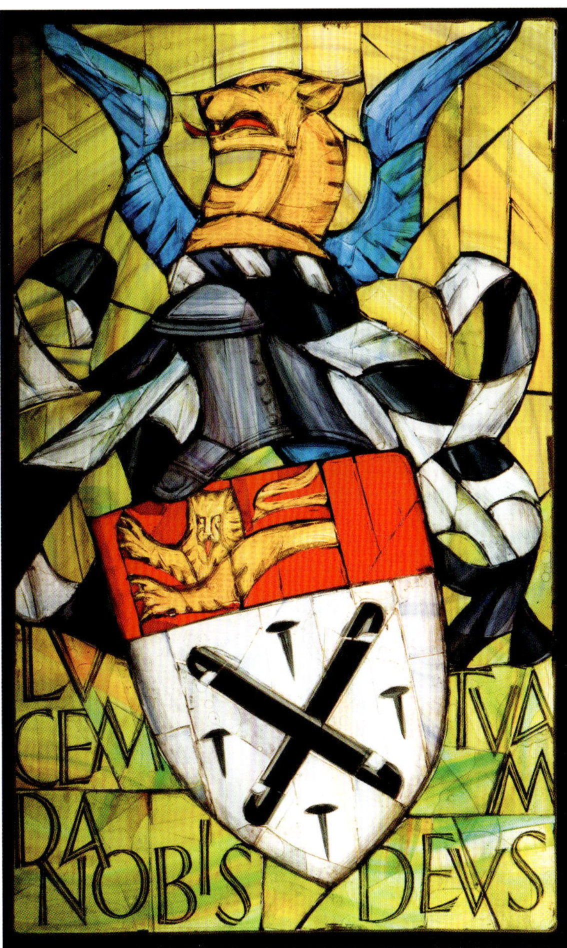

THE ARMS OF THE WORSHIPFUL
COMPANY OF GLAZIERS *c.*1973
Designed and made by Moira Forsyth
(1905–91)

The arms of the Worshipful Company of
Glaziers feature the tools of the glazing
craft: two grozing irons and glazing
nails. The Livery Company existed as
early as 1328 and thrives today, with a
number of practising artist craftsmen
among its members.

Moira Forsyth trained as a potter
before turning to stained glass design
after seeing the medieval windows of
Chartres Cathedral. Much of her working
life was spent at the Glass House in
Fulham. This panel was made using a
modern appliqué method in which one
piece of glass is bonded to the surface
of another with adhesive in a stained
glass equivalent to collage. The relative
impermanence of these adhesives
makes appliqué windows unsuitable for
conventional architectural settings.

*From the artist's studio. Donated by the
artist's estate, 2014.* (1982.8)

A LIVING ART: CONTEMPORARY STAINED GLASS

Although today traditional methods of making stained glass have changed little since the medieval period, new technologies as well as changing tastes have transformed approaches to the use of coloured glass in buildings over the last fifty years. Techniques such as fusing, sandblasting, casting, engraving and etching have developed alongside new printing and laminating technologies. These have allowed a greater variety of stained glass art than ever before. New materials, together with rapid developments in artificial lighting, digital and computing technologies, have presented new opportunities for artists. Stained glass thus remains one of the most dynamic and inspiring art forms of the 21st century. Although many of the large studios that once employed artists and craftsmen have closed and few art institutions teach stained glass today, a number of skilled artists continue to work in this medium. Contemporary architecture offers new structural as well as aesthetic opportunities for this light-transmitting art form, while the ongoing restoration of stained glass in important heritage buildings ensures its continued appreciation and provides much work for specialist conservators.

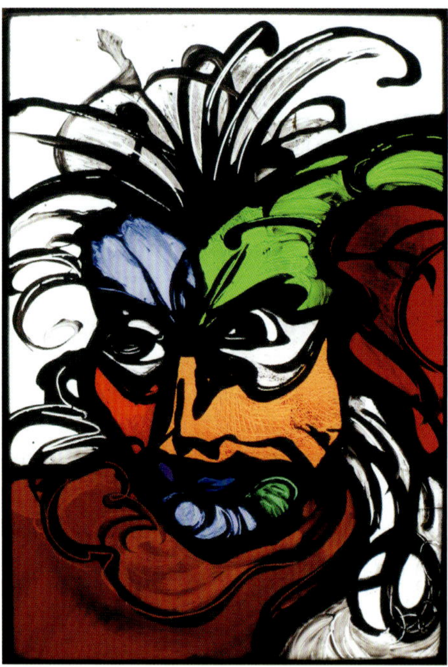

ONE WOMAN'S NARRATIVE: SELF PORTRAIT IV 1994
Designed and made by Debora Coombs (born 1956)

This autobiographical panel was made for Coombs's first solo exhibition at the Jeanette Cochrane Theatre in London in 1994. Based on childhood memories, this series marked the beginning of a figurative phase in Coombs's work, combined with the geometry and decorative pattern that characterised her earlier pieces. Although born in Britain, Debora Coombs now lives in the United States. She has exhibited widely on both sides of the Atlantic.

From the artist's studio. Donated by the artist, 2015. (1998.1)

INNER SPACE 1979
Designed and made by Paul San Casciani (born 1935)

The descendant of an Italian master cabinetmaker, Paul San Casciani trained at Whitefriars Glass and is an author and teacher of stained glass. This panel was designed to illustrate the many techniques of the craft, including acid-etching, tracing and water-spotted matt, double plating, copper foiling and traditional leading, opalescent, appliqué and fused glass. The design, based on an electron photomicrograph of the hydra, a micro-organism, demonstrates how science provided inspiration for stained glass artists in the late 20th century.

From the artist's studio. On loan from the artist, 1987. (L1987.1)

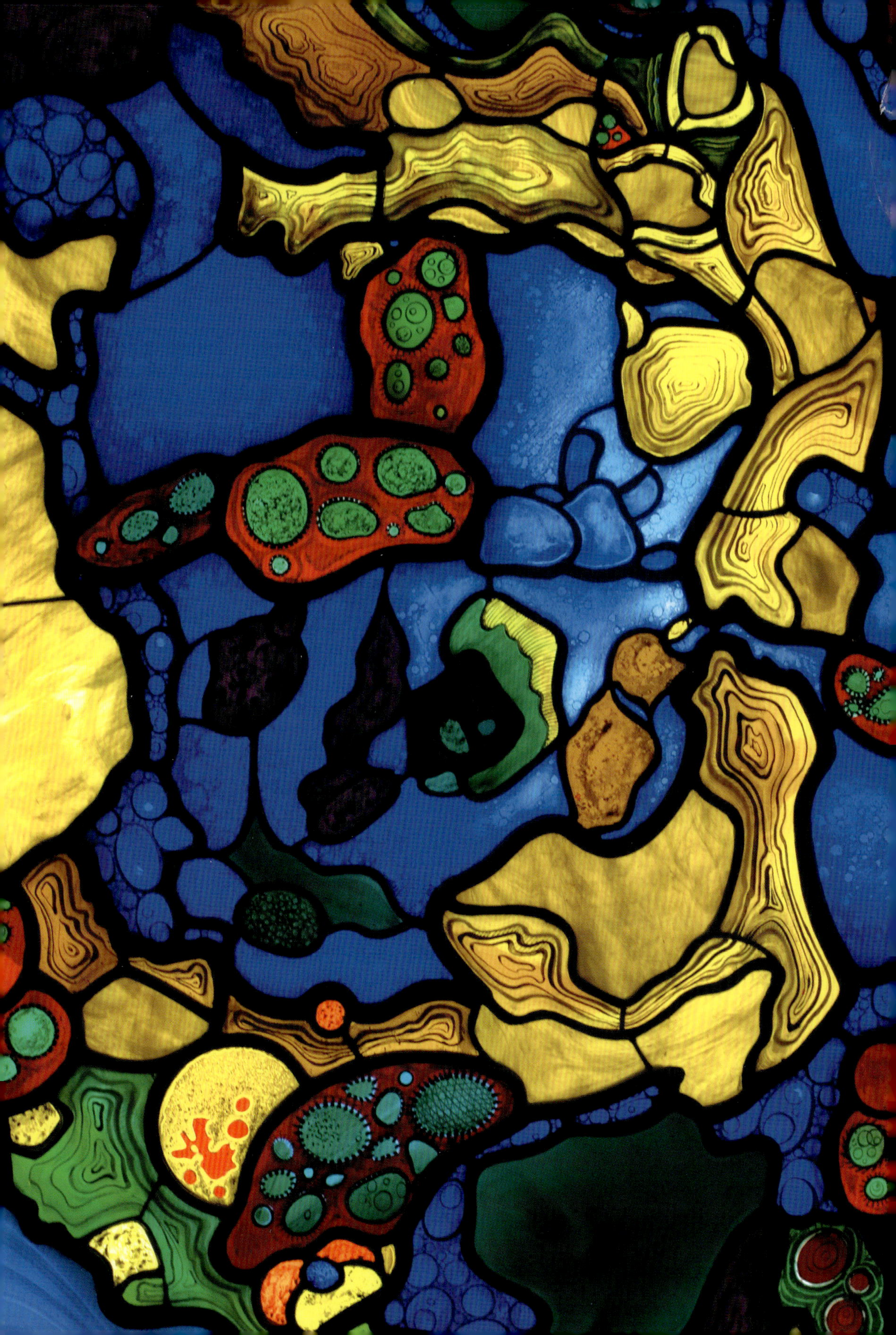

Designed and made by Rosalind
Grimshaw (born 1945)

Different representations of violence
from turbulent political events in
recent history are brought together
here in a complex composition using
a variety of stained glass techniques.
Pieces have been etched with acid,
stained, plated and leaded to
juxtapose different textures and
tones. The imagery reflects a number
of stories to be contemplated
individually or as a combined
statement on the theme of violence.

Rosalind Grimshaw trained in
the stained glass studio of Joseph
Bell & Son in Bristol under Geoffrey
Robinson until his retirement in 1996.
She then opened her own studio and
won the commission to design and
create the Millennium Window for
Chester Cathedral.

*From the artist's studio. On loan from
the artist, 2007.* (L2007.4)

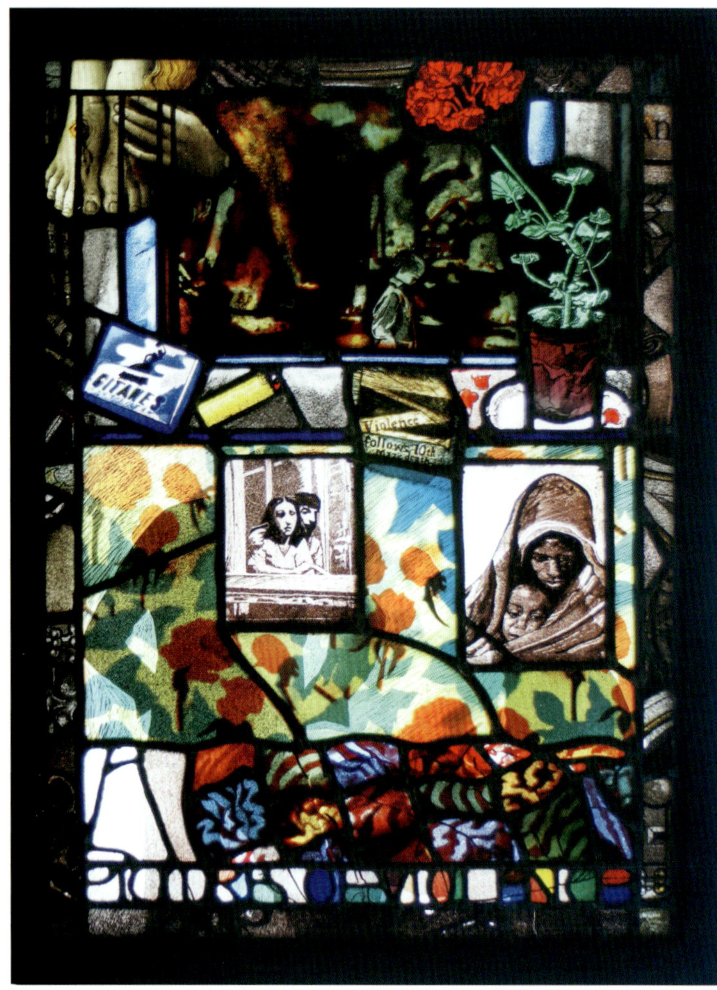

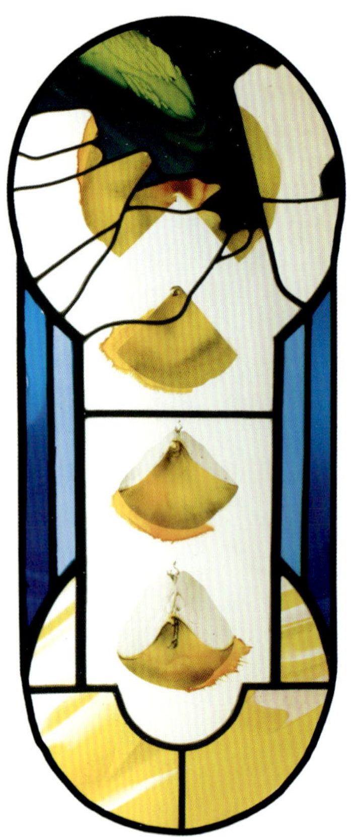

METAMORPHOSIS 1979
Designed and made by Albinas
Elskus (1926–2007)

Produced as an exhibition panel,
this work shows the artist's
fascination with still life. Apples,
the 'forbidden fruit', are the focus
of this semi-abstract panel, which
reveals the artist's mastery of
glass painting technique. Elskus
trained first in his native Lithuania
and then studied architecture
in post-war Germany before
emigrating to the United States in
1949. He was a leading exponent
of traditional glass painting in
America.

*From the artist's studio. Donated by
the artist, 1996.* (1996.6)

OPPOSITE
THE TEMPTATION OF
ST ANTHONY c.1980
Designed and made by Patrick
Reyntiens (born 1925)

St Anthony led a strict ascetic life
as a hermit. He was tormented by
hallucinations in the form of demons
and erotic visions, which he resisted
with prayer. Reyntiens has employed
a variety of techniques in this panel,
including acid-etching and plating, to
dramatic effect. As well as interpreting
the designs of John Piper in stained
glass, Reyntiens is one of Britain's
most respected stained glass artists.

*From the artist's studio (exhibition panel).
Purchased with a grant from The Keatley
Trust, 1999.* (1999.1)

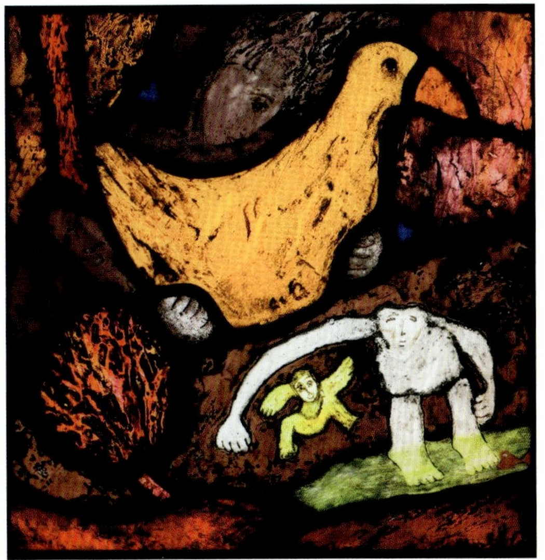

SURE ENOUGH THE DUCK 1992
Designed and made by Peter Young (born 1962)

This whimsical panel illustrates a number of characters
in the mid-point of a story. Peter Young was born and
studied in Dublin. After taking a diploma in Visual
Communication Design, he moved to London, developed
a fascination for stained glass and enrolled at the Central
Saint Martin's College of Art and Design; he returned
to Dublin in 1996. Young has received a number of
commissions since the 1990s for schools and churches.

From the artist's studio. Donated by the artist, 2014. (1992.5)

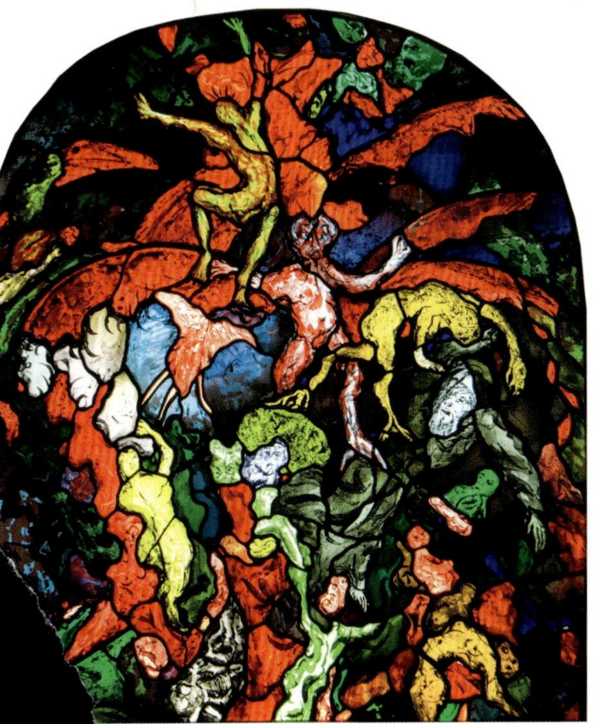

THE PEEL COTTAGE WINDOW 1982
Designed by Brian Clarke (born 1953); made in
Derix Glasstudios Taunusstein, Germany

The son of an Oldham coal miner, Brian Clarke is
today one of the leading exponents of architectural
stained glass in Britain. Inspired by the work of
German artists such as Johannes Schreiter, Clarke
has worked consistently in an abstract geometric
style, often on a vast scale, winning international
acclaim and commissions from Riyadh to Rio de
Janeiro. Notable commissions in the UK include
collaboration with Sir Norman Foster at Stansted
Airport and an enormous glazed arcade over the
Victoria Quarter in Leeds, described by Clarke as
'an unending flow of liquid colour'.

*From Peel Cottage, Kensington, London W8.
On loan from the artist, 2000.* (L2000.2)

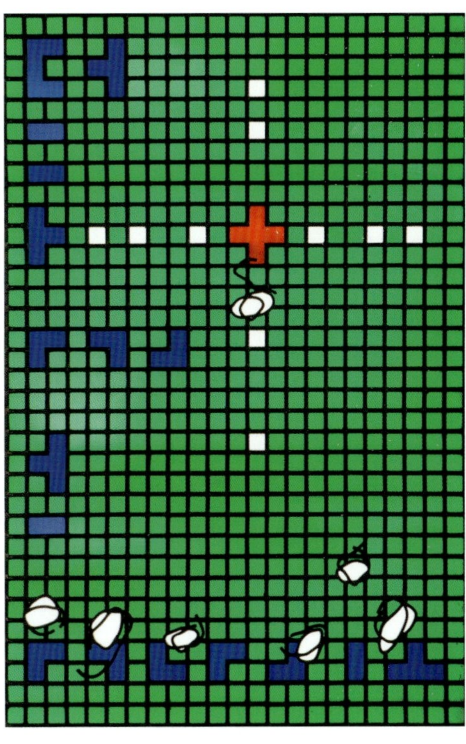

GLOSSARY

ACID-ETCHING
The process of removing the surface layer from flashed glass to expose the underlying glass. This is achieved today by using hydrofluoric acid. In the medieval period an abrading tool was used.

ANTIQUE GLASS
Mouth-blown hand-made glass.

CALME
From the Latin *calamus*, meaning reed, H-shaped strips of lead used to assemble the pieces of glass. It is composed of a central part, the heart or core, with leaves or flanges covering the edges of the glass. Originally cast in moulds, in later times lead calmes have been extruded through a lead mill.

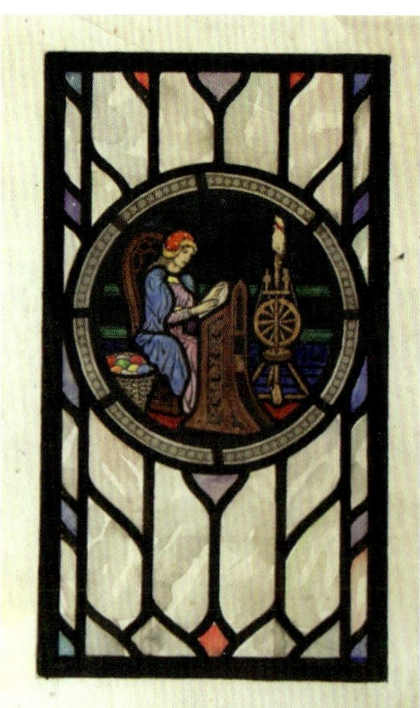

CARTOON
The full-sized drawing of a stained glass window to show the exact size and shape of all the pieces of glass, their colour, the sizes of the lead and the support system required to glaze the window.

CEMENT
Used to make a panel completely watertight once the window has been leaded together. Made from a mixture of whiting (powdered and washed white chalk), linseed oil and fixative, it is spread over both sides of the glass with a brush. The glass is subsequently cleaned with sawdust or whiting that soaks up any surplus cement.

COPPER FOILING
A technique in which individual pieces of glass are surrounded by copper tape, laid edge to edge and soldered along the join.

CROWN
A disc of mouth-blown glass. Pieces blown by this method are recognisable by the concentric striations that result from the spinning of the crown during its manufacture.

DALLE-DE-VERRE
A technique which uses pieces of coloured slab glass set in a matrix of concrete or epoxy resin.

DESIGN BELOW
The artist's first sketch for a stained glass window, generally in a ratio of 1 to 10. Usually coloured, the design is used as the basis for the full-size cartoon. Historically it was called a 'vidimus'.

ENAMEL
A powder of coloured pot metal glass frit (a mixture of silica and fluxes) that can be diluted and used for painting many colours on glass. It is fixed by firing at temperatures between 550°C and 750°C.

FERRAMENTA
The metal framework (iron, aluminium, copper, brass) fixed into the masonry to hold panels of stained glass.

FLASHED GLASS
A base sheet of glass, usually white, on which is overlaid a thin 'flash' layer of coloured glass. The coloured layer can be ground away to reveal the clear or white glass underneath.

GATHERING
The action of taking a ball of molten glass, known as the 'parison' or 'gather', in order to blow it.

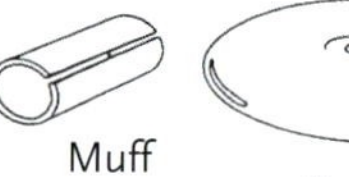
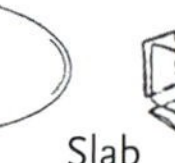
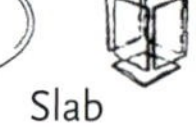

GLASS ABOVE
In the case of stained glass, the glass is blown and manipulated into a muff, crown or slab bottle.

GLASS PAINT
A brown or black-coloured vitreous paint used to paint on glass, made from a mixture of finely ground glass, iron or copper oxide, and a flux. It is fixed to the glass by firing at around 650°C.

GRISAILLE
From the French word *gris* meaning grey. A delicate pattern, usually of foliage, is painted onto white quarries that are then made up into geometric windows using very little coloured glass.

GROZING
A method of shaping the edges of pieces of glass to the right size using a metal tool known as a grozing iron.

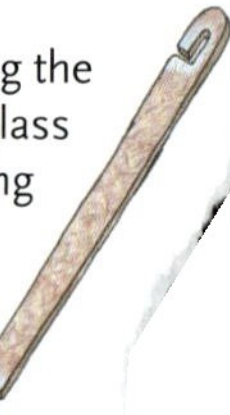